WE DON'T PLAY WITH
GUNS HERE

Debating Play Series

Series Editor: Tina Bruce

The intention behind the *Debating Play* series is to encourage readers to reflect on their practice so that they are in a position to offer high quality play opportunities to children. The series will help those working with young children and their families in diverse ways and contexts, to think about how to cultivate early childhood play with rich learning potential.

The *Debating Play* series examines cultural myths and taboos. It considers matters of human rights and progress towards inclusion in the right to play for children with complex needs. It looks at time honoured practices and argues for the removal of constraints on emergent play. It challenges readers to be committed to promoting play opportunities for children traumatized through war, flight, violence and separation from loved ones. The series draws upon crucial contemporary research which demonstrates how children in different parts of the world develop their own play culture in ways which help them to make sense of their lives.

Published and forthcoming titles:

Holland: *We Don't Play With Guns Here*
Hyder: *War, Conflict and Play*
Kalliala: *Play Culture in a Changing World*
Manning-Morton: *A Time to Play: Playing, growing and learning in the first three years of life*
Orr: *My Right to Play: A Child with Complex Needs*

WE DON'T PLAY WITH GUNS HERE

War, weapon and superhero play in the early years

Penny Holland

Open University Press
Maidenhead · Philadelphia

Open University Press
McGraw-Hill Education
McGraw-Hill House
Shoppenhangers Road
Maidenhead
Berkshire
England
SL6 2QL

email: enquiries@openup.co.uk
world wide web: www.openup.co.uk

and

325 Chestnut Street
Philadelphia, PA 19106, USA

First published 2003

A catalogue record of this book is available from the British Library

ISBN 0 335 21089 9 (pb) 0 335 21090 2 (hb)

Library of Congress Cataloging-in-Publication Data
Holland, Penny, 1955–
    We don't play with guns here : war, weapon, and superhero play in the
    early years / Penny Holland
        p. cm. – (Debating play)
    Includes bibliographical references and index.
    ISBN 0–335–21090–2 – ISBN 0–335–21089–9 (pbk.)
    1. Play. 2. Child psychology. 3. Children and violence. 4. Toy guns –
Psychological aspects. 5. Education, Preschool – Great Britain. 6. Day care
centers – Great Britain. I. Title. II. Series.

    HQ782 .H65 2003
    306.4'81 – dc21

                                                                    2002030372

Typeset by RefineCatch Limited, Bungay, Suffolk
Printed in Great Britain by Biddles Ltd, www.biddles.co.uk

This book is dedicated to the memory of my brother, Alan Randall Holland, who died shortly before I embarked on the research on which it was based. The close relationship we developed during his illness and the conversations we had during that time are directly connected to the changes in my thinking which underpin this work.

If I have not yet learned to love Darth Vader, I have at least made some useful discoveries while watching him at play. As I interrupt less, it becomes clear that boys' play is serious drama, not morbid mischief. Its rhythms and images are often discordant to me, but I must try to make sense of a style that, after all, belongs to half the population of the classroom.

(Paley 1984: xii)

CONTENTS

SERIES EDITOR'S PREFACE

The Debating Play series is not intended to make comfortable reading. This is because 'play' is not a comfortable subject. For a century at least, play has been hotly debated among researchers, practitioners, parents, politicians and policy makers. Arguments have centred around whether it should have a place in any childhood curriculum framework. Its presence in schools and other institutions and settings has ebbed and flowed according to who holds power, influence and authority to control curriculum decisions.

When play has been permitted in settings, it has often suffered from a work/play divide. Play in such contexts is frequently confused with recreation. However, an alternative approach is to offer 'free play', through which children are thought to learn naturally. This works well in mixed age groups (2–7 years) when older, more experienced child players act as tutors and initiate younger children, helping them to learn through their play. Sadly, though, this is rarely experienced in early childhood settings in the UK nowadays. It is noteworthy, however, that a few nursery schools have managed, against great odds, to keep an age range from 3–5 years and research (Siraj-Blatchford *et al.* 2002) indicates that the learning children do through their play in these settings is rich.

There is a growing understanding of the importance of play as diverse evidence accrues, which highlights the role of play in early learning in relation to ideas, feelings, relationships and movement (embodiment). However, this is often mistakenly interpreted as adults showing children how to play, through guiding, tutoring, role-modelling or whatever name is of current fashion, rather than providing children with genuine opportunities to engage in their *own* play.

The intention behind the Debating Play series is to encourage readers to reflect on their practice so that they are in a position to offer high quality play opportunities to children. The series will help those working with young children and their families in diverse ways and contexts, to think about how to cultivate early childhood play with rich learning potential.

The Debating Play series examines cultural myths and taboos (such as weapon and super hero play). It considers matters of human rights and progress towards inclusion in the right to play for children with complex needs. It looks at time honoured practices and argues for the removal of constraints on emergent play. It challenges readers to be committed to promoting play opportunities for children traumatized through war, flight, violence and separation from loved ones. The series draws upon crucial contemporary research which demonstrates how children in different parts of the world develop their own play culture in ways which help them to make sense of their lives.

The Debating Play series is evidence based rather than belief driven.

Each book in the Debating Play series probes an aspect of play. In this volume, Penny Holland looks at the contentious issues surrounding weapon play.

Penny Holland has established both a national and international reputation for her work researching weapon play in early childhood settings. She re-examines the 'belief' based approach of zero tolerance of weapon play. Her research, with the full participation of parents, staff and children, makes a challenging and thought provoking read. The result is a book with the message that when adults stop attempting to control children's emerging understandings of war, aggression, peace and justice, citizenship, negotiating acceptable outcomes, they help children to learn. Supporting young children so that they learn through their play seems to lead to children to consider moral issues in depth.

There are many myths to be challenged in this area of early childhood play. Is it only boys who indulge in weapon play? Should children be given weapon replicas to play with? If not, is it acceptable to let children make their own weapons and to use them in the play scenarios they create? Should all weapon play be banished, or is this one of the ways in which young children begin to think and deal with violence, injustice, power, despotism, aggression, peace, war and the world we live in?

Penny Holland asks readers to dwell and reflect upon the mounting evidence which suggests that there needs to be a major review of current practice, and the way adults support children's play to allow them opportunities for deep thinking. The book helps those working with young children and their families to develop the kind of engagement through play which leads to educated, informed and moral responses to the violence and aggression that exists in the world.

I commend this book to you.

Reference

Siraj-Blatchford, I., Sylva, K., Mittock, S., Gilden, R. and Bell, D. (2002) *Researching Effective Pedagogy in the Early Years*, Research Report 356, Department for Education and Skills.

Tina Bruce

PREFACE

War, weapon and superhero play is a controversial, under-researched and under-theorized aspect of children's play, which is rarely discussed in an open-minded way.

For approximately the past 30 years early years settings and primary schools in England have operated a zero tolerance approach to this area of play. This means that children are not allowed to bring manufactured toy weapons into settings, are not allowed to construct weapons from construction, technology or found materials, and are not allowed to enact scenarios associated with superhero, war or play-fighting. This ban is often extended to incorporate other forms of noisy, physically active play like chasing and running games. This area of play is almost exclusively associated with boys.

Support for this policy rests on a belief that there may be a connection between children's early involvement in aggressive play themes and the development of aggressive behaviour.

As a parent and early years practitioner I supported this approach to war, weapon and superhero play, believing it to be consistent with my feminist and pacifist principles, and I enforced this approach rigorously.

In the spring of 1998 two events sparked against each other to cast a different light on my personal and professional perspectives on this area of play. First, co-workers at the under-fives centre where I worked in inner London made me aware of the negative impact that my rigorous approach was having on one particular child and together we then started to observe how our collective prohibitive approach was affecting a small group of boys in our class who had a persistent interest in war, weapon and superhero play. No matter how rigorously we tried to outlaw this play some children would persist.

We noted that they were receiving a disproportionate amount of negative attention and that our interventions were affecting their well-being and self-esteem. They were not engaging in other activities in a sustained way, often looked crestfallen after these interventions, and were prone to disruptive behaviour following them.

The second contributing event was becoming aware that colleagues at a pioneering centre of excellence were moving towards relaxing zero tolerance by allowing sword play. While following wholesale the example of those we respect is not a course of action I would advocate, I do believe that we need to be open and to reflect on the innovative practice of our peers in the early childhood community.

As practitioners in a low-status area of education we often undervalue our ability to research and develop our own practice. We tend to feel that theory and research of value only resides in the realms of large-scale quantitative or statistical samples or in the words of dead, white men. We also tend to expect this research to be interpreted for us by experts in early childhood, the intermediaries in the academic chain. We rarely engage directly with this research material and even more rarely do we feel that we can challenge such material or conduct our own research to test those theories which influence us. At the time these two events coincided I was studying for an MA in Early Childhood Education with Care, and it was probably the demands of this course which gave me the confidence and context to combine these two events into a piece of action research.

In brief, we decided to relax our zero tolerance approach, to allow children to construct weapons and enact superhero and conflict scenarios. We monitored the ensuing play and behaviour carefully and noted significant benefits to those children who had a persistent interest in this area of play. At the end of the research period all practitioners in the setting agreed that a return to zero tolerance could not be justified and that the benefits of working actively with these play themes far outweighed any difficulties we had encountered in the process of making this change.

When I began to disseminate these findings through articles and workshops it became clear that many practitioners were feeling uncomfortable with the policy and practice of zero tolerance and a number of settings embarked on their own action research in this area. In order to develop an evidence base of changing practice I began both to collate the findings from these settings and to work alongside a smaller group of settings to support their practice and to observe the impact on children's play of changing practice in those settings. This work is ongoing and I do not claim that the findings presented in this book offer conclusive or definitive evidence about the effects of relaxing a zero tolerance approach to war, weapon and superhero play in early years settings.

I do claim, however, that the findings offer a unique insight into the possible benefits of relaxing this approach and that they provide sufficient evidence to prompt a major review of policy and practice in this area and point to the need for further small-scale practitioner-based action research and larger scale longitudinal research on this issue.

This book shares aspects of the journey of personal and professional development undertaken by practitioners in the setting where my initial research took place, by those who had embarked independently on that journey and those influenced by the positive findings from my earlier research. The book equally gives weight to the voices and experiences of the children directly affected by the changes in the attitudes and approaches of these practitioners.

These developments are contextualized in an examination of the historical genesis of a zero tolerance approach and of key theoretical perspectives in the area of gender and imaginative development, as well as specific theoretical perspectives on war, weapon and superhero play. These perspectives are then reviewed through the particular experiences of settings where zero tolerance has been relaxed. In this way theory and practice are linked throughout the book.

I hope that readers will see the book as offering new ways of reading war, weapon and superhero play specifically, as well as a validation of the important role that small-scale action research by practitioners in early childhood settings can play in expanding our knowledge, understanding and responses to children's play.

My intent is not to change minds, but rather to open them and to fuel debate within the early childhood community in relation to zero tolerance of war, weapon and superhero play, which I believe has become a stagnant area of policy and practice.

ACKNOWLEDGEMENTS

The leading 'thank-you' in this list acknowledging those whose support has made this book possible must go to the children and practitioners, whose play and professional practice form the heart of my work. In order to guarantee their anonymity, given the potentially controversial nature of some of the material contained in this book and possible media interest, it is not possible to name them. The practitioners know who they are and I thank them for their insight, courage and commitment to developing practice in the area of war, weapon and superhero play to serve the best interests of the children in their care. I hope this book gives them and the children they work with a voice in the wider early childhood community.

Thanks must next go to Tina Bruce as my mentor and editor. Her unstinting support and 'critical friendship' have ensured both that this book was safely birthed and that I survived the experience intact and with a now established view of myself as a writer.

Although I had been granted a sabbatical from the University of North London to support the writing of this book, I would not have been able to take full advantage of this opportunity without the direct support and intervention of my close colleagues, Merryn Hutchings, Linda Pound and Julia Manning-Morton. Their generous practical and moral support has been central to the successful conclusion of this project and I can't thank them enough.

Last, but most definitely not least, acknowledgements are due to those who have suffered most while I have been writing this book: my mother Kath; my daughter Frania and my partner Carol. Their support has been the most important because it is their love for me and their pride in my achievements that has kept me going. Thanks to them for believing in me and for putting up with my being physically present but mentally absent.

ZERO TOLERANCE OF WAR, WEAPON AND SUPERHERO PLAY: WHERE DOES IT COME FROM AND WHY DO WE DO IT?

It is close to the beginning of a session in a nursery classroom. Most of the children have arrived and they are settling down to their chosen activities. Out of the corner of her eye an early years practitioner, Gina, spots two boys on the other side of the room playing suspiciously in the construction area. There are no other adults close by. Fred is toting a gun crudely assembled from two pieces of Lego. He takes aim at Hakim, who is crouching behind an enclosure of hollow blocks they have just built together. Hakim is holding a small curved unit block; there is no mistaking from his pose and the way he holds it that in his mind it represents a gun. They are smiling. Simultaneously they cry out 'peow, peow, peow' and start to chase each other in a circle around the enclosure. Gina has by this time crossed the room and gently, but firmly, reminded the two boys that 'We don't play with guns here. Guns hurt people. We're all friends at nursery and we don't like to hurt each other, do we?'

The boys shake their heads, but Hakim summons the courage to protest, 'But we're only pretending.' Gina raises her eyebrows 'But it's not nice to even pretend to hurt someone, is it?' She doesn't pause for a response before adding her concluding comment, 'Why don't you go and do a painting instead?'

I wonder what they would have said had Gina allowed them to answer her rhetorical questions, or had she questioned them about their desire to pretend to shoot?

Fred and Hakim decline her suggestion about painting and wander around aimlessly for a while, both looking a little crestfallen. Neither child settles down to another activity and they are the first on with their coats as soon as the doors to the garden open. Once in the garden they quickly assemble two guns from the Lego pieces they managed to stash in their pockets on the way out and run off to the quietest, least visible corner. Their game continues, but this time they are careful to keep their shooting sounds low and half an eye on adult movements.

This time when Gina approaches they are prepared: one of the guns magically becomes a drill and the other a mobile 'phone. Gina raises her eyebrows knowingly at the children, but is secretly relieved that she will be spared her routine intervention on this occasion. She colludes with their inventive lie, but feels honour bound to remind them that they are not allowed to take Lego into the garden and tells them to take it back inside. The smiles are wiped off their faces and their shoulders hunch in compliance as they do as they are told.

In another corner of the garden a group of four boys, Anton, Joseph, T.J. and Omar, are playing Power Rangers. They strike poses, deliver a few karate kicks and chops into the air and then chase off after each other in a circle around the climbing frame. They stop and run the fight sequence again. Anton receives an accidental kick on his shin, but after his friends comfort him the play resumes. Meanwhile, another child, Robert, who is not involved in the play, has taken it upon himself to tell Gina that they are playing the banned game. She approaches the group sternly: 'I am fed up with having to tell you about this. I had to speak to you yesterday. We don't play Power Rangers at nursery. When you kick and punch someone might get in the way and get hurt. And anyway, it isn't nice to fight like the Power Rangers. Now you two go inside and do some writing and the others can find something else to do. I don't want to have . . .' She is interrupted by the cries of a child who has fallen off a bike and badly grazed an elbow.

A zero tolerance approach to war, weapon and superhero play will be all too familiar to most early years practitioners in this country and the scenes described above are typical examples of that approach. A zero tolerance approach means that children are not allowed to bring toy weapons into settings, are not allowed to construct or represent them with found materials and are not allowed to enact war play or superhero scenarios.

The scenes described encapsulate the seeds of the range of issues that lie at the heart of this book: female practitioners' perception of war, weapon and superhero play; the impact of zero tolerance on the well-being and development of those boys who show a persistent interest in war, weapon and superhero play; and the fact that zero tolerance simply doesn't work in terms of eliminating this play from early childhood settings. At best it works to suppress the play and some would argue that it at least discourages those with a less persistent interest from pursuing such play. However vigorously practitioners enforce a ban on this area of play, some children, almost exclusively boys, will persist with making and using pretend weapons and enacting superhero scenarios. This means that practitioners are trapped into expending a great amount of negative energy in policing boys' play to enforce the approach.

The volume of this persistent play will vary from setting to setting and from year to year depending largely on the presence of individual or small groups of boys with this interest and on the dynamics that develop around them. The play rarely disappears altogether and if it does it is generally only for a short time, usually until a new intake of children arrives. Such an approach seems on occasion to offer little more than a cushion to beat off the many-headed war, weapon and superhero play monster. No sooner have you dealt with one head than another pops up behind you.

Why then have we persisted with what seems to be such an inadequate approach for so long, and why did we wish to ban such play in the first place? Many elements of early childhood practice come to be seen as business as usual: we go on doing them but we don't remember, or perhaps we never knew in the first place, why? Unless something or someone stops us in our tracks we often simply carry on doing what we have always done. Also in recent years the agenda for policy review and change in early childhood has largely been set by external agencies like Ofsted, the Qualifications and Curriculum Authority (QCA) and local authorities, and the time and encouragement to reflect on issues outside those agendas has been limited.

Nevertheless, my work in this area of play, which has involved me in dialogue with hundreds of practitioners from all sectors of early years provision, has made two points abundantly clear: zero tolerance is overwhelmingly the prevalent approach to war, weapon and super-hero play in England; and large numbers of practitioners are beginning to find this approach inappropriate and inadequate. This also appears to be the case internationally as evidenced by a number of papers considering aspects of the debate from Australia (Cupit 1996), Greece (Doliopoulou 1998), the USA (Carlsson-Paige and Levin 1990, 1995), Italy/UK (Costabile et al. 1991), as well as England (Broadhead 1992).

An historical perspective

Zero tolerance, in common with all areas of early childhood practice, can be placed in a historical and theoretical context and in this chapter we will explore that context in the hope of developing a shared understanding of current practice.

One of the most striking features of the history of zero tolerance is that there is no paper trail to follow. I have yet to find a setting which has a written policy or policy statement concerning this approach. Nor have I found such guidance in local authority documents.

I began to search for such documentation both in order to substantiate my own understanding of how zero tolerance came to be so prevalent, and also in response to the language and rationales I had heard bandied around in various staff rooms over time in justification of zero tolerance. In essence these consistently referred to zero tolerance as the product of an earlier local authority or Inner London Education Authority (ILEA) policy. It should be noted that the complexity of such a search is partly rooted in the complex history in the UK of early years provision itself (Smith 1994; Moss and Penn 1996).

To summarize, public sector early years provision historically has developed from two roots: education and care. Local education authorities have had responsibility for nursery schools and classes; health authority and then social services have overseen provision within day care settings. In addition a substantial amount of provision is made within the voluntary and private sectors, which, although they can be described as independent, have nevertheless been influenced by local authority guidance, particularly since the considerable changes in registration and inspection processes required by the 1989 Children Act.

As most of my research was carried out in inner London, searching for policy documentation is further complicated by the fact that social services departments have always been organized on a borough basis, while education was organized London-wide under the umbrella of the ILEA until 1990 when it was devolved to the boroughs. There is no independently catalogued ILEA archive, and successive reorganizations within social services departments have rendered their archive material similarly inaccessible. Searches of catalogued local authority documents and ephemera have produced nothing relevant to this area of policy.

As an alternative research strategy I decided to speak to some of the inspectors and senior advisers who had been working within the ILEA early years sector during the 1970s and 1980s. I was successful in contacting four of these, who between them had held senior central early years posts between 1975 and 1990, when the ILEA was closed down. They all asserted that there had been no written policy document on this specific area of play, while three out of the four suggested that the general feeling was that such play should not be encouraged.

The fourth was shocked to hear that zero tolerance had gained ascendancy as an approach and, contrary to the other three, did not agree that a level of zero tolerance would have been common during her time at the ILEA, from 1977 to 1986, although this overlapped with the time served by two of the other three. She felt that such a position would have contradicted the post-Plowden child-centred approach current at the time. All felt that this would not have been an area considered suitable for detailed policy consideration, and commented that written policy was not as prevalent 'at that time' as it is now. One had a memory of attending a conference at which toy gun play was discussed, and of writing a paper for the British Association for Early Childhood Education based on the conference, but could not narrow this down within the 1975–85 time frame. Another contact, who had been an ILEA nursery school head during the 1960s and 1970s, reported that she could recall a memo being sent out by the authority between 1967 and 1969 which stated that no school funds should be used to purchase toy guns or weapons. I have not, however, been able to track such a document down.

The sort of search that I have just been describing is clearly a search for a single, simple historical account, a 'metanarrative' or 'grand narrative' (Lyotard 1984: xxiv) rooted in modernist concepts of absolute, objective, rational truths.

Even had such a search proved more fruitful I am not sure how much the identification of an authoritative voice would have illuminated our understanding of both the genesis and tenacity of zero tolerance. It would only have given us part of the picture: policy is Janus-like in that it looks both backwards and forwards; reflecting and projecting concerns and intentions. It would probably be more illuminating to seek out these concerns and intentions, and I propose to do this in a pluralistic way by considering the individual biographies, in relation to zero tolerance, of seven practitioners, whose experiences are representative of the many with whom I have spoken. This approach to teasing out the historical context of zero tolerance acknowledges that there is no single story to tell.

> From a post-modern perspective, there is no absolute knowledge, no absolute reality waiting 'out there' to be discovered. There is no external position of certainty, no universal understanding that exists outside history or society that can provide foundations for truth, knowledge and ethics. Instead, the world and our knowledge of it are seen as socially constructed and all of us, as human beings, are active participants in this process (Berger and Luckman 1966), engaged in relationship with others in meaning making rather than truth finding.
>
> (Dahlberg *et al.* 1999: 23)

The practitioners' years of experience within early years settings range from 15 to 26 years and cover social service, voluntary sector and educational settings in London, Sheffield, Nottingham and Liverpool. Five of them reported that zero tolerance had been in place for the last twenty years of their practice and had been equally prevalent in social services, education and the voluntary sector, regardless of geographical location. Two practitioners reported that zero tolerance had become more prevalent over the last fifteen years. None remembered receiving any input on war, weapon and superhero play during their initial Nursery Nurse training, but the same group of five identified above all described receiving clear messages concerning zero tolerance in the early days of their first jobs, from either teachers or managers. This came in the form of instructions to 'distract or discourage'. None could remember ever being presented with a written policy relating to this area of play and it was described as an 'unwritten rule'.

Two practitioners chose to comment that they had not questioned the approach. They had felt that the manager knew best and so they went along with it. While issues of status and power in relation to the determination of practice in the early years are evident in these accounts, i.e. the assumption that Nursery Nurses or unqualified staff will act in accordance with practice defined by teachers or managers, compliance alone does not seem to offer a sufficient explanation of the tenacity of zero tolerance, even in the two accounts highlighted above. If these two practitioners had been asked to comply with practices they felt to be bizarre, dangerous or otherwise unacceptable it would be reasonable to assume that their comments would have encompassed some kind of disclaimer like, 'I didn't agree with it, but I had no power to change it.' I believe that, in common with the other five practitioners, such an approach made sense to them at some level of their experience.

I will now look at some of these accounts in more detail to identify a number of strands which I believe will help to contextualize a zero tolerance approach, and show how practitioners have been agents in keeping this approach in place.

One practitioner, who has 26 years' inner London experience, felt that she could identify a change in practice in the mid-1980s, which related to in-service training concerned with anti-sexist practices in the early years. She had very clear memories of the term 'Wendy house' being highlighted in these sessions as an inappropriately gendered name for which 'home corner' should be substituted as an anti-sexist option. She remembered war, weapon and superhero play being discussed in these forums, with zero tolerance being presented as the correct approach, with Barbie dolls for girls being included in the ban. Although this practitioner earlier described zero tolerance as 'an automatic thing; I just went along with it', her subsequent reflection revealed a far greater sense of agency. She had felt that zero tolerance 'made sense, common sense; we shouldn't be encouraging violence'. Her memories mesh with events which can be externally validated as they coincide with the publication of a number of key documents in relation to anti-sexist practice, which were supported by training activities (Whyte 1983; ILEA 1985, 1986). Interestingly, none of the documents cited above specifically refers to war, weapon or superhero play, but clearly in this practitioner's experience it was discussed in the above context as an example of sexist play.

The next account is similar to the above, except that the practitioner had always, during 22 years, worked in settings with a zero tolerance approach, and had never encountered change or related in-service training. She describes her own personal views as having been influenced by the approach to the extent that she would not allow her own children to engage in war, weapon and superhero play. Over time the approach came to make sense to her in relation to adult male violence and an understanding that 'if you give in to kids it's like you're agreeing'. She thus became a more active agent in promoting zero tolerance.

Two of the practitioners described far stronger personal experiences, which enabled them to make explicit connections with the zero tolerance approaches they had consistently encountered during their careers in early years, in both cases going back twenty years in settings in London and other cities. Both described personal involvement in the peace movement, anti-Vietnam war demonstrations and Campaign for Nuclear Disarmament (CND) marches from the late 1960s through to the 1980s. One had grown up with her father in the forces, always seeing adult males dressed in uniform, and being allowed to sit in fighter planes in their hangars. She had reacted against these military influences in the context of popular protest available to her in her teens.

The second practitioner identified an early experience of being with her Polish grandmother, who had witnessed both her parents being shot in front of her during the German occupation of Poland during the Second World War. Her grandmother would always switch off the television if a violent programme or news item came on. She described becoming involved with friends who were active in the peace movement during her teens and then participating herself. She also described working with victims of domestic violence as being a significant influence, as was having a network of gay male friends, who presented her with an alternative construction of masculinity. Both had felt that zero tolerance was consistent with their personal philosophies of peace and had upheld the approach as a proactive intervention in the early expression of male violence. The connection did not have to be scientifically established; as with the previous practitioner, the connection seemed to be self-evident or made common sense.

These last two stories have resonance with my own. My previously rigorous support for zero tolerance was rooted in my involvement with the women's liberation movement from the mid-1970s to the mid-1980s. My concerns were with male violence in its more domestic forms, that is, domestic violence and rape.

During the late 1970s and early 1980s male violence – domestic, sexual, institutional and military – became a major focus for feminists, both nationally and internationally, as witnessed by the following non-exhaustive list of campaigning and action groups active at that time: Women Against Violence Against Women; Women Against Rape; Rape Crisis; Women's Aid Federation; Reclaim the Night; Women Against Imperialism; Greenham Common Peace Camp. In seeking to make sense of the spiral of male violence debate also raged between those who took a more biologically deterministic view and those who felt nurture had a larger part to play. In relation to toy gun, weapon and superhero play the response would have been the same. Take the gun away because it already acts as an expression of male violence and confers power, or take the gun away and give them dolls and more peaceful toys instead so that they can be socialized away from models of violence at an early age.

I am choosing to focus here on discussions and debates that were taking place within informal grass roots feminist forums, such as consciousness-raising groups, conference workshops and activist meetings, as opposed to the academic feminist context. I believe that, although such debates and discussions are difficult to evidence and reference, it is important to cite them here as they involved thousands of women from a diverse range of backgrounds and informed academic feminism. I would argue that it was this mass movement of women (the Women's Liberation Movement) that had a more significant effect on public debate and attitudes at the historical juncture being considered than academic feminism, which developed subsequently as a meaningful body of work.

Grass roots feminists at that point were not concerned with making scientifically proven links, even had that been possible, but were more concerned with making sense of the global spiral of male violence and to intervene directly wherever possible in the chain of connection they identified. Lived common experiences and intuitive analysis were effectively utilized and respected as a counterpoint to the patriarchal, scientifically rational arguments which historically had been wielded against women, such as, if you can't prove it in our terms it's not a valid argument.

Indeed, one could summarize this counter-logic as stating that just because something can't be proved does not mean it isn't true. Feminists were engaged in raising a number of hypotheses in relation to the causes and effects of male violence based on empirical evidence. Violence is not experienced theoretically and the need to act in immediate ways to intervene in the spiral took ascendancy over the need to elicit scientific proof of cause and effect. Perceived sexist patterns in children's play clearly presented themselves as an area in which women could take some control.

The movements I have identified can be seen as having a major role in generating zero tolerance approaches. They are an expression of the zeitgeist, or spirit, of the 1970s and early 1980s.

The last account I wish to mention is that of one of the most experienced practitioners with whom I have spoken, which provides a reminder that the zeitgeist to which I have referred has a pedigree longer than that already identified. This practitioner was born at the beginning of the Second World War and relates her personal abhorrence of war, weapon and superhero play to this fact.

Reflection: keeping an open mind

I have dwelt on these narratives because it has become clear to me that zero tolerance is more to do with individual practitioners' experience, attitudes and feelings than a carefully thought out approach to an area of play. This emerges consistently from discussion with practitioners at workshops concerning war, weapon and superhero play. I have dwelt on these personal narratives because it has become clear that in order to consider war, weapon and superhero play more openly practitioners must often suspend their personal views.

> Making individuals conscious of the discourses they encounter and the positionings they experience is one of the most radically empowering moves possible. Or, to look at it another way, the real power of hegemonic discourses is the power of the familiar, the habitual, of positionings accepted without conscious thought . . . Individual subjects are basically the prey of dominant discourses if they are not aware of other discourses and the positionings they construct.
>
> (Cranny-Francis 1992: 14)

In order to be reflective practitioners and to develop practice which has sound pedagogical foundations, I believe we must be prepared to examine our own stories and to interrogate those most deeply held moral convictions which can make us deaf to the needs and understandings of children. We must bring greater depth to our understanding of that seminal early years principle of 'decentre-ing' (Donaldson 1978: 25), as the following quote implies specifically in reference to educators' moral positionings:

> The individual needs of students may be ignored in teachers' crusades to realize their personal visions . . . It seems that the moral self-assurance we assume in our practices and reinforce in our self-descriptions is dangerous, not least because it creates a situation where our actions are sanctioned by an unquestionable moral arrogance informing our teaching. As teachers, we can make the assumption that because we are guided by high moral values, our practices must inevitably operate in the best interests of the students. Seen from this perspective, change seems unnecessary and even immoral. Consequently, our teaching and our secure moral identities become fixed, and the student must adjust. This inability to change is compounded by the self-assuring autobiographical style in which we incorporate ourselves unambiguous narratives. As long as we teachers become located – and thus locked – in our stories, the possibilities for alternative interpretation, for reflexivity and for self-criticism are greatly reduced.
>
> (Convery 1999: 140)

War, weapon and superhero play and aggression: is there a connection?

From the perspectives I have outlined my view is that zero tolerance practices are not explicitly based on any hard evidence of a causal connection between early toy gun, weapon and superhero play and the development of aggressive behaviour, but rather on a common-sense, nurture-based belief that there might well be, and that no harm could be done by acting on that assumption. While few practitioners make specific reference to theory or research supporting this assumption, many believe that such research exists and supports a zero tolerance approach. I will conclude this chapter with a brief examination of some of the strands of research which relate to this area of play in order to see whether this belief has any substance.

My investigations have revealed little trace of research specific to war, weapon and superhero play from the 1970s, 1980s or 1990s which either explores or proves such a connection. As Watson and Peng (1992: 370) observe:

Although many parents and others interested in child welfare suspect that allowing children to play with toy guns may have deleterious consequences in increasing their general aggression, little research is available on which to draw any conclusions.

Sutton-Smith (1988) reviewed eight pieces of related research extant in the late 1980s. Three of these purport to demonstrate no effect on levels of aggressive play from exposure to war toys and five to demonstrate some effect. Sutton-Smith concludes that the research methods employed in all eight studies are flawed for a number of reasons, some of which are common to all the studies. The most commonly cited criticisms are that the studies fail to distinguish between play-fighting and real aggression, they do not take into account the impact of novelty in relation to the toys introduced, presence of researchers or change of routine, nor do they consider other social variables in relation to the children being observed. The studies are also based on short periods of observation; some were conducted in laboratory situations; and observations recorded are vulnerable to observer bias. None of the studies are longitudinal and they focus solely on considering a connection between toy gun play and aggressive behaviour in an immediate time frame. None of the studies are in fact designed to establish cause and effect and at best indicate toy gun use as a significant variable when children are observed to behave aggressively.

> The major conclusion to these eight studies ... is that they are all unreliable pieces of work. It is not possible on the basis of this body of work alone to conclude anything for certain about the relationship between war toys and aggressive behaviour. In areas of human behaviour as subtle and as critically important as this, we should conclude nothing that is not clearly replicated in a number of studies.
>
> (Sutton-Smith 1988: 64)

Turner and Goldsmith (1976), the authors of one of the studies cited as establishing a connection between toy guns and aggressive behaviour, based their study on the immediate and contrasting effects on children's free play of playing with a toy gun or aeroplane. While their analysis showed a statistically significant increase in aggressive play after children had played with toy guns, the actual incidence of aggressive events was minimal. In addition, increased aggressive play was also noted after children had played with the toy aeroplanes. The data on which their conclusion was based was evidently tenuous.

Neither did they consider the long-term effects of playing with aggressive toys.

A more recent piece of research was conducted in the early 1990s by Watson and Peng (1992). They videotaped 36 children between 3 and 5 years old (19 girls and 17 boys) in a day care setting in Boston, USA. Their free play behaviour was then coded for evidence of real and pretend aggression, rough and tumble play and non-aggressive pretend play and the results correlated with information from parental questionnaires concerning frequency of play with toy guns, levels of physical punishment, and levels of aggression in children's preferred TV programmes and toys. They concluded:

> Multiple regression analyses indicated that amount of parental punishment strongly predicted real aggression in both boys and girls, and amount of gun play strongly predicted real aggression in boys . . . These results indicate that toy gun play and parental punishment are positively associated with a higher level of real aggression but not pretend aggression.
>
> (Watson and Peng 1992: 370)

This research does not seem to move us significantly closer to being able to describe a causal link between toy gun play and aggression. At best it indicates that aggressive children like to play with guns, but more importantly it signals that children's experience of real aggression, in the form of parental physical punishment, translates into aggressive behaviour towards others.

Perhaps it is significant that the centre in which Watson and Peng conducted their research does not allow toy gun play. One might speculate that the children who play with toy guns at home and are observed as using real aggression and less pretend aggression are doing so because they are not allowed to use their chosen fantasy material in the day care setting. In addition, we have no indication of the levels of imaginative play used by children while playing with their toy guns at home. In short, the clearest contribution of this piece of research is to point us in the direction of children's other more direct experiences of aggression and violence in the hunt for causative explanations of how aggressive behaviour develops.

Finally, I will refer to a more recent piece of work (Orpinas *et al.* 1999) which, although concerned with older children, does build interestingly on the previous paper discussed in that it considers 'Parental influences on students' aggressive behaviors and weapon carrying'. The research involved a survey of 8865 middle school students between the ages of 12 and 14 in Texas in order to ascertain whether a connection could be made between family structure, relationship with parents, parental monitoring, perception of parental attitudes towards fighting and the aggressive behaviours and weapon carrying of the young people surveyed.

The analysis of the survey revealed a correlation between higher aggressive and weapon-carrying behaviours and poor parental relationships, low parental monitoring, perceived high parental support for fighting and not living with both parents. However, 'perceived parental communication about fighting had the strongest effect on the students' aggression' (Orpinas *et al.* 1999: 785). This 'perceived parental communication' was indicated by selecting from such phrases as 'If someone asks you to fight, you should try to walk away', 'If someone asks you to fight, hit them first.' The research findings imply that young people receiving the latter sort of advice from parents are more likely to be involved in aggressive behaviours. This is comforting confirmation for practitioners, who are aware anecdotally of the difficulties that arise from managing the challenging behaviour of children who respond to advice to 'talk it through' by saying, 'But my mum/dad says I should hit back.'

Clearly it is impossible to make a definitive connection between this research and the previous example (Watson and Peng 1992) as they consider children from very different age ranges and the former presents data on parental attitudes to fighting, while the latter considers actual physical punishment of children. However, it is perhaps not unreasonable to read a common message from parents to children across these different sets of data. Young children receiving physical punishment at the hands of their parents are as clearly being given the message that it is acceptable to hit others as the older children receiving that information verbally from parents.

Although causative connections are difficult to prove, both sets of research strongly suggest that parental messages about physical aggression are potentially influential on children.

Whether or not a clear causative link between toy gun play and the development of aggressive behaviours can be proved, I would suggest that past assumptions about such a connection or trying repeatedly to establish such a link is possibly a red herring. Establishing such a link would do little to inform practice beyond confirming zero tolerance as an appropriate strategy, whereas practitioners are clearly not finding such an approach helpful.

An alternative hypothesis suggested by my own research is that zero tolerance in fact inhibits us from supporting the development of other imaginative and negotiating skills, which may mediate the real risk factors present in those children's lives in relation to aggressive behaviours.

It is clear that extant research into war, weapon and superhero play is overwhelmingly concerned with the effects of the artefacts associated with this area of play, which are measured in limited time frames, and does not concern itself with the role of the practitioner or the possibility of working with children to mediate these effects.

Conclusion

In this chapter I have looked at the political, moral and theoretical backdrop to a zero tolerance approach to war, weapon and superhero play. I have argued that the roots of this approach cannot be traced through policy documents and that they lie in the pacifist and feminist movements of the 1960s, 1970s and early 1980s. The perspectives of these movements have influenced practice both directly through the personal histories of practitioners and more indirectly through the philosophies of those who have trained and managed them. By looking at various strands of evidence concerning the link between experiences in early childhood and the development of aggressive behaviour I have challenged the view that we can draw a simple connection between war, weapon and superhero play and aggression. Such a connection is implicit in a zero tolerance approach. While the sincerity of practitioners' desire to intervene in the spiral of male violence cannot be challenged, I have argued that such 'common-sense' arguments should be replaced by reflective practice with practitioners looking carefully at the impact of zero tolerance on the children in their care.

2

BOYS WILL BE BOYS AND GIRLS WILL SIT NICELY

Any discussion of war, weapon and superhero play will almost inevitably turn into a discussion about gender. The most obvious reason for this is that the majority of children who are seen to take an interest in making and playing with weapons are boys: a perspective shared by early years practitioners and parents internationally in Australia (Cupit 1996), Greece (Doliopoulou 1998), the USA (Carlsson-Paige and Levin 1990, 1995), and Italy/UK (Costabile *et al.* 1991), as well as in England (Broadhead 1992).

Such discussions tend to focus on the question of why boys have an interest in weapons and aggressive and violent play themes and will almost certainly return to the well-worn debate about whether gender role behaviour arises from nature or nurture. These debates also presuppose that war, weapon and superhero play can be viewed as a discrete area of play, which can and should be viewed differently to all others.

I resist such a circumscribed notion of war, weapon and superhero play and will argue in later chapters that in order to understand and work with this aspect of children's play we need to look beyond the weapons to the play themes which lie beneath the surface. Discussions in this chapter will also incorporate the impact of practitioners' understandings of and attitudes towards the gender culture in early childhood classrooms and zero tolerance as a significant aspect of this practice.

While the nature/nurture debate will be addressed in this chapter we will be considering a line of argument that will suggest that the debate has not been resolved in the scientific world and cannot be resolved in relation to early childhood practice. I believe our approach to gender relationships in early years settings over the past twenty years has served to harden rather than challenge stereotypical behaviour. This approach is characterized by the corrective and sometimes punitive form of response offered to active young boys in counterpoint to the celebratory response given to compliant and passive young girls playing in the home corner or at the writing table. Both of these responses should cause us equal concern.

We will link this argument to the historical perspectives explored in Chapter 1 which suggest that a zero tolerance approach to war, weapon and superhero play arises more from practitioners' personal rather than professional understandings of the development of male violence.

In order to begin to illustrate this point let us return to the series of interactions between Fred, Hakim and Gina at the beginning of Chapter 1. We see two small boys intercepted and thwarted twice in their attempts to pursue a taboo play theme despite their creative lies designed to throw the adult off the scent. They have not hurt anyone, they have asserted the difference between fantasy and reality (not that anyone appeared to be listening to them), they are playing companionably together, and yet their play attracts only negative attention from the adult, female practitioner. The boys are described as crestfallen. The practice of zero tolerance is acted out at this interface of age, gender and power.

I will be arguing that girls are as vulnerable as boys at this interface. I will look at the impact of zero tolerance on girls' play and question the traditional assumption that girls are just not interested in weapons or play fighting. The common link across these gender themes is perception: how children see themselves in relation to gender and how others see them.

The nature/nurture debate revisited

It would not be possible to rehearse here the whole range of arguments in relation to whether gender role behaviour arises from nature or nurture. The issues and lines of argument do need to be summarized, however, because some practitioners see the persistence of war, weapon and superhero play across time and place as evidence of innate biological differences: boys will be boys. Indeed, such statements seem to be coming back into more common use after some years in the wilderness. They arise to some extent from a sense of despair, that after twenty to thirty years of concerted attempts to promote equal opportunities between boys and girls one can look around most nursery classrooms and see the same gendered grouping of play preferences: girls in the home corner; boys on the construction carpet.

These feelings are also fuelled by the continuing escalation of male violence in the adult world. It is possible to draw support for such perspectives from a range of 'scientific' sources (Kimura 2000; Gurian 2001) which assert that substantial differences can be identified between boys' and girls' brains, which impact on rate and patterns of development. However, even within such texts caution is urged in terms of drawing hardline conclusions about the impact of these differences on behaviour and life experiences. Kimura notes this in the conclusion to her book, which otherwise emphasizes experimental evidence of gender differences in brain development (Kimura 2000: 182–3):

> Keep in mind that many of the tests that demonstrate consistent sex differences, are employed for that very reason. That is, they are probably relatively 'pure' ability tests, meaning that they have minor overlap with other tests. However, in the world outside the laboratory, most of our activities involve a mix of abilities. This means, potentially, that performance on pure tests may not predict performance very well on a variety of real-world activities . . . Moreover, most of the tests we discussed in this book are time limited . . . Unquestionably, if unlimited time were given, men's and women's scores on some tasks would approach or equal each other.

She is thus acknowledging that the effects of any gender-related brain specialism might be mediated by the complex interactions demanded by real-life tasks.

Other writers in the current field of neuroscience like Susan Greenfield (1997, 1999), who espouse a less reductionist perspective, emphasize this complexity even further and take a more holistic view of brain development and function. This view gives prominence to the interplay between experience and the plasticity of the child's developing brain (Greenfield 1999: 2):

> The balance between nature and nurture seems to swing in favour of nurture as the brain becomes more sophisticated, and less emphasis is placed on instinct and more on individual experience – and hence in the growth of individuality. The brain is enormously 'plastic'; only now is work really revealing just how sensitive the brain is to reflecting all experiences. It is no exaggeration to say that you have a unique brain, not in the shape of the macro regions, but in the configuration of the micro-circuitry.

Another area of scientific argument used to explain gender-differentiated development of behaviour is the role of hormones. While the role of androgens and oestrogens pre and post-natally and at adolescence in determining sex differentiation is not contested, there is considerable debate about the role of testosterone in relation to displays of aggression in young boys. Steve Biddulph (1997), who urges the acceptance of gender-differentiated behaviour on biological grounds, suggests that boys at approximately 4 years old experience a testosterone surge which accounts for an escalation in aggressive behaviour at that age.

This view is contradicted by other scientific writers (Rose *et al.* 1972 and Travis and Wade 1984, both cited in Head 1999) who argue that testosterone is not a priming hormone in relation to aggressive behaviour but is found in enhanced quantities after an aggressive encounter. In the wider scientific field there is considerable ongoing debate about the precise relationship between testosterone and aggression, with the connection being associatively but not causally proved. A survey of the literature indicates that few studies have been conducted with young boys and that the conclusions from these studies are subject to debate within the scientific community.

Clearly there are no simple conclusions to be drawn in relation to gender role behaviour from scientific sources. The greatest difficulty anyway with any biological arguments is that they fail to account for the great diversity of non-stereotypical behaviour among both boys and girls. Significant differences in behaviour within gender reaffirm that gender role behaviour is socially acquired. Practitioners commonly report that only a small group of boys, often just four or five in a class of 25, will stand out as having a significant interest in weapons and play fighting. With encouragement and adult presence many girls will absorb themselves with skill and ingenuity equal to the boys in construction activities.

While I am asserting that biological differences cannot account for gender role behaviour, it is important to emphasize that I am not suggesting that biology has no part to play. Kohlberg (1966) argued that it is when children achieve gender constancy – an understanding that their sex is genitally, i.e. biologically, determined, even though at this point they do not view it as a necessarily permanent state of affairs – that they begin to interact with the range of information available to them in relation to what it means to be male or female. Nor, indeed, would I venture to argue that the experience of growing up in a body biologically engineered for different reproductive functions and with growth promoted by different hormonal influences does not impact on our experiences of, or our view of, the world. I would argue, however, that those experiences have a greater influence later in childhood and adolescence.

Sources for the early meaning making referred to by Kohlberg are myriad: parents/carers; siblings; grandparents; peers; television; books; packaging; early years practitioners, and so on. The value-laden content of that understanding will vary depending on the child's family culture and peer group influences.

One of the features of this process, which I feel we often misinterpret in early years settings, is the presence of stereotyped behaviours and perceptions, which many, although not all, children commonly display while they are struggling to make sense of what it means to be a boy or girl. What is also crucial to note here is that children are not responsible for the nature of gender role messages available to them. This may seem to be an obvious point, but it is one I think we sometimes forget in our dealings with children when, as parents/carers or practitioners, we react harshly or impatiently to the extremes of gendered behaviour we encounter when it does not match our espoused ideal.

In developing their gender identity there are clearly a number of entrenched stereotyped models of behaviour and appearance available to children, especially in the media: adverts during children's TV slots are the most glaring examples of this. These may include toy preferences, pink/blue colour discrimination, hair length, play styles and emotional displays. Children at this point in the process of forming gender identity are seeking certainty; they are trying to find a rule or rules that will make them feel that they belong in the gendered world that surrounds them. What is impossible to map is how these different and often contradictory influences gain ascendancy for individual children. There are no straight connecting lines to be drawn on this map. Children who have been brought up in anti-sexist homes are just as likely to exhibit stereotyped behaviour as children brought up with more traditional gender roles and vice versa.

Whatever influences children respond to in their search to make sense of their gender identity they will often seek to make them universal. I am reminded here of the way in which young children will over-generalize rules in language like the use of 'ed' endings for the past tense: I goed, I sleeped. It is this struggle to make sense that leads children to make those statements: boys don't play with dolls; girls can't play firemen; girls don't have short hair, often in the face of contradictory experience, which can send practitioners running back to biological explanations of gender role.

Ellen Jordan (1995: 75–6), in her discussions of how young boys construct masculinity, considered a view of masculinity being defined as 'not feminine' and concluded:

It seems that these boys have adopted a definition of masculinity in which the subordinate term is the behaviour of females, that being male is primarily doing things that cannot and should not be done by women.

(Jordan 1995: 75)

She extended the analysis to suggest that boys adopt this discourse as a fall-back position lest they fail to establish credibility within the 'warrior discourse' (Jordan 1995: 76), and that this offers them another tangible framework within which to make sense of their gender. It could be argued from this that when zero tolerance is in operation some boys are being prevented from exploring one avenue of gender identity open to them – war, weapon and superhero play – and are forced to adopt the fall-back position described above. In two settings, where zero tolerance was relaxed and boys received positive affirmation for interests they perceived as male, some boys were able to move beyond their fall-back position and cross the boundaries to explore areas previously considered taboo by dressing up in feminine clothing. This transgression in turn become absorbed into the realm of possibilities for boys' behaviour, i.e. boys can explore anything. The risk-taking behaviour displayed by these boys also impacted on the gender discourses available to other boys in the class and many of them joined in with the exploration of dressing up and associated role-play.

This border crossing behaviour was also noted by Kate Pahl (1999: 94) in her observations in an early years classroom headed by a male teacher where war, weapon and superhero play themes were accepted and respected: 'Boys frequently took on "female" identities as if this were the norm. It was as if, because they had a comfortable male role model, the boys could explore identity without inhibition.'

I believe that a better understanding of the possibility of and reasons for stereotyped gender behaviour could have a significant impact on how practitioners view and interact with children around issues of gender. There has been a tendency, perhaps, to view children displaying stereotyped behaviour as being or having a problem. The problem is not theirs, but ours.

The moral panic with which we sometimes react to the gender stereotyped behaviour of young children can sometimes lead us to have a blinkered view of the actual and potential fluidity of the range of apparently contradictory gender identities which children can take up, often simultaneously. I have frequently witnessed young boys in the throes of quite aggressive war, weapon and superhero play scenarios suddenly step out of role to comfort or seek help for an injured or upset child whom they have encountered (the injury or upset not being a consequence of their play). They are demonstrating an ability both to distinguish between fantasy and reality and to cross the borders of stereotyped gender behaviour. I believe such moments, which challenge oversimplified readings of gender behaviour, are often missed by practitioners, either because they interact with the play only to stop it or because they steer clear of it as it disturbs them, or they feel they have nothing to learn from it.

The shift of understanding that I believe is necessary would also challenge a somewhat simplistic equal opportunities approach to gender which presupposes that it is sufficient to challenge those gender stereotypes we see as negative and positively reinforce those behaviours we see as positive. What I believe we may have failed to take account of is that by simply challenging these stereotypes in a negative way we are challenging children's growing sense of self at a delicate point of development.

'Girls are nicer than boys'

Before exploring this point further I would like to raise a glaring imbalance in the way such stereotypes are perceived and challenged. Which stereotyped behaviours attract the lion's share of our attention? Do we focus equally on the quiet, passive, domestically orientated play that occupies so much time for so many young girls? Do we feel concern about the impact on their physical development of an excess of sedentary activity? Are we concerned that their compliance to the routines and rules of the classroom may signal a more worrying compliance to a passive female role in the future? Many practitioners agree that they do little to shift young girls' horizons beyond settled and sedentary activities because these do not cause them any management difficulties.

Most of our negative attention in relation to gender-stereotyped behaviour is directed at the lively, noisy and physical play associated with some boys of which war, weapon and superhero play is a prime example. The following list may serve as a reminder of the many different ways we say 'no' to those boys; most could apply to any form of active play:

You know we don't play like that at nursery:
    because we don't want any of you to be hurt;
    because we don't want you to hurt each other;
    because we don't want you even to pretend to hurt each other;
    because we don't want you to disturb the other children;
    because you are here to learn;

  because guns hurt people;
  because it's noisy;
  because we want you to do a nice painting for mummy;
  because you boys would never do anything else;
  because it isn't nice;
  because I don't like it;
  because I said so.

Clearly sex identity, the knowledge of being a boy or a girl, features significantly in the development of a child's early self-image, so it is important to consider the impact of our negative interventions on that development.

> Side by side with the development of self-image the child is learning that there are ideal characteristics he/she should possess – that there are ideal standards of behaviour and also particular skills, which are valued.
>
>   (Lawrence 1988: 4)

It is not unreasonable, then, to conjecture that a child would be selecting gender-related characteristics in this construction of ideal self. As suggested above, these characteristics will be drawn from a number of sources and may be contradictory. Let me illustrate this by looking a little more closely at Fred and how he may experience Gina's consistent rejections of his play interests.

Fred's story

Fred lives in a conventional heterosexual two-parent family. Both parents work full-time and are equally involved with the setting. Fred seems to have a much stronger attachment to his father, who regularly takes him to the park to play football or to the swimming pool at weekends. Fred is, however, on extended day provision (from 8am to 5.30pm) and during the week he will regularly go home to watch the latest Disney video. His father is also a member of a gun club, collects antique guns and displays them at home. These interests are all present in his play at the setting and it is not, therefore, unreasonable to suppose that these elements are present in his ideal self-concept firmly attached to his developing gender identity.

  So what happens to his self-esteem and gender identity when we reject, however kindly, the model of a cannon, like the one in the fireplace at home, that he has so carefully constructed? I realize that what follows is conjecture, but it is offered as a possible rather than certain description. Fred understands that he is male, like his dad, to whom he is attached and with whom he identifies and is a major source for his construction of ideal self. As he is on extended day provision acts of representation, which bring precious but absent realities into his present, are especially important. These representations not surprisingly include his father's favourite artefacts, guns, which are taboo in the setting. Practitioners, operating within zero tolerance, perceive his representations as signs of dangerous masculinities, an idea I will return to later in the chapter. Fred perceives his representations as comforting reminders of home and as an expression of his maleness.

Fred's dad is not a violent man. He doesn't use his guns to shoot people; he shoots at targets. The characters in Fred's cartoons aren't real; they are 'just pretending', like him. His ideal self is a little boy who would like to have adventures like the characters in his cartoons and who makes beautiful models of cannons and guns.

When we reject his efforts on the grounds of an ideological and theoretical connection with real violence how do we expect him to make the connection? What connections might he be making instead? 'Boys like guns and cannons and having adventures. You say they are bad things, so does that mean boys are bad? I'm a boy; am I bad? My dad likes guns. He's a boy; is he bad? I'm always a boy; am I always bad? You only say nice things to me when I do the things that girls do.'

Not only do we hijack his attempt to move towards his ideal self, which would raise his self-esteem, but also our actions suggest that his ideal self and associated maleness are undesirable. In doing so we make it impossible for him to enhance his self-esteem. Lawrence (1988: 5–6) observes that

> Failure in a particular area generalizes so that he/she would not just feel a failure say in reading attainment, but will feel a failure as a person generally. The child is not able to compartmentalize his/her life as can the adult . . . The child with low self-esteem . . . will lack confidence in his/her ability to succeed. Consequently, he/she may try to avoid situations which he/she sees as potentially humiliating.

I am not trying to suggest that every small boy deflected from making a gun has suffered irreparable damage to his self-esteem. I am concerned about the cumulative effect of repeated interventions of this sort on the handful of young boys with a burning preoccupation with war, weapon and superhero play. Often such children are hard to engage in other activities and will positively shun anything resembling 'formal' learning. Often, as previously pointed out, such prohibitive responses from practitioners towards young boys are also extended to any form of active or noisy play most frequently favoured by boys. It would not be unreasonable for early childhood practitioners to reflect on whether such negative messages contribute to the early alienation and disaffection that seem to be disadvantaging some boys within the educational system. Chapter 3 will further tease out the possible implications of this in relation to imaginative development.

Drawing on my analysis of Fred's experience I would suggest that perhaps we need to take a more radical and more pragmatic approach to understanding adults' role in constructing gender in early years classrooms. Whatever combination of biology and social construction (nature and nurture) gives rise to the preference shown by some boys for war, weapon and superhero play and/or other forms of active and noisy play, practitioners have a professional responsibility to work with those boys and their play in a way which does not generate low self-esteem or negative gender identity, as illustrated by Fred's story.

Let sleeping girls lie

I will now return to an exploration of how such prescriptive responses to gendered behaviours creates a genderscape in the early years classroom which can limit the options for both girls and boys. Girls are receiving equally strong messages into their ideal self files about sedentary, passive and stereotyped domestic play and toys like Barbie dolls. While many settings have adopted a parallel ban on girls bringing Barbie dolls into settings, as we had, the nature of play being promoted to girls is far more readily translated into the activities already on offer in early years settings. This play was recreated using available dolls in the home corner, markers for nail varnish etc., and because it was peaceful and presented no management problems it did not attract the same negative attention as the stereotyped boys' play.

In addition, because the girls were receiving general validation for being quiet, settled and cooperative, their self-esteem was being fed, their gender identities were not being challenged and perhaps as a result of this they had the confidence to engage with a wider range of activities. This would include those activities less problematically associated with boys, like construction and block play, in which we had little difficulty in promoting an interest when we used simple strategies like getting down on the carpet ourselves.

Our success did not extend, however, to those activities more closely associated with gross motor skills and the use of the vocal cords – in other words, the kind of activities often connected with boys engaged in war, weapon and superhero play and related physically active play. I would suggest that this is hardly surprising given the levels of negative attention directed at boys trying to engage in such activities. Physically active play was clearly highlighted as a no-go area and, given the benefits of well-being accrued from compliance to a passive and cooperative female gender schema, there appears to be little incentive for girls to challenge this status quo.

To illustrate this point it may be useful to consider the phenomenon of the 'tomboy'. This expression is significant, first in the way it is used by adults to describe girls behaving in a non-stereotypically feminine way as a reflection of a discourse which limits the border crossing possibility for girls by labelling any adventurous, assertive and physically active behaviours as male. Second, such a discursive practice serves to make some girls who are determined to pursue these behaviours feel that they have to relinquish their identity as a girl in order to do so. Such a girl might be thinking: 'Girls have long hair, wear dresses and sit around in the home corner playing with dolls; I want to run around and play superheroes and football; I don't want to be like a girl, I want to do boys' things so I'll have to give up girls' things.' To be both lively, active and female will present itself as an untenable position to many young girls. Francis (1998: 46), drawing on Walkerdine, summarizes this point succinctly:

> . . . there is no position for girls to take up as active child: they can take up the position of 'feminine object of masculine gaze', or of quasi-teacher . . . Girls who do not conform to this behaviour are often penalised more heavily by teachers than are boys . . . naughty girls are 'little madams'.

This point is also explored by Diane Reay (2001) in her examination of the femininities available to young girls, which identified four key categories of 'Spice Girls', 'Nice Girls', 'Girlies' and 'Tomboys'. She notes that 'Implicit in the concept of "tomboy" is a devaluing of traditional notions of femininity, a railing against the perceived limitations of being female' (Reay 2001: 162).

On the other hand we have a significant number of young girls fighting to defend the elevated position of 'good girl' by colluding with us in Othering some of those little boys. They would be the first to come and report any transgressions against zero tolerance while it was in force; they would exclude boys from the home corner unless they complied with the roles they allocated to them; and they would make generalized statements about the boys' behaviour, for example, 'the boys are always naughty', or 'the boys always fight'. The following extract of comments made by children in an American kindergarten suggests this is not an uncommon feature (Paley 1984: 26).

Karen: Girls are nicer than boys.
Janie: Boys are bad. Some boys are.
Paul: Not bad. Pretend bad, like bad guys.
Karen: My brother is really bad.
Teacher: Aren't girls ever bad?
Paul: I don't think so. Not very much.
Teacher: Why not?
Paul: Because they like to colour so much. That's one thing I know. Boys have to practise running.

I believe that one of the effects of this is that in Othering 'boyish' behaviour – and I believe I have indicated that zero tolerance has in practice encompassed most forms of physically active play – we were understood by children only to value the passive and quiet activities generally associated with girls.

To appreciate the impact of this aspect of practice it is helpful to note what can happen when zero tolerance is relaxed. As with the example given earlier of boys crossing the borders of stereotyped gender behaviour, similar risk taking was witnessed in some girls. When the play themes were sanctioned, and female workers were seen to join in with the adventure scenarios that arose, girls' participation proliferated. It seems for them too that the relaxation of zero tolerance and the sensitive involvement of staff in developing what followed increased the range of possibilities of what it might mean to be a girl. During a recent conversation with the head of the centre, where the original research was conducted, she observed that the team is now more consistently witnessing children playing in mixed gender groups.

This raises the question, therefore, of the extent to which, in our efforts to decommission the perceived armoury of incipient male aggression, we have narrowed the gender identity options for both boys and girls. In this process do we not also sanction and engender that female passivity which is the corollary of male violence? A common anxiety expressed by practitioners about relaxing zero tolerance is that it might result in the intimidation of young girls by boys playing aggressively. An alternative approach, which is discussed at length in Chapter 5, is the empowerment of all children to resist play and behaviour that they dislike.

While non-violent conflict resolution is a personal ideological tenet, and one which I believe has inspired zero tolerance historically, I wonder if under-developing children's physical strength, agility and experience of their own physical power helps or hinders this project? My understanding of the philosophy underpinning the more ancient Japanese martial arts is that one learns to fight in order that one doesn't have to. The connection I am making is that when conflict-ually related, active play scenarios are sanitized out of our early years settings, with the message to children that these are only negatively associated with boys, we are preventing girls from understanding that resistance is an option and boys from understanding that girls can be active and resistant. I think we need to reflect in far greater depth on the passivity we are engraving on girls' bodies as a result of policing young boys' behaviour in order to protect them.

Blinkered perceptions

In Chapter 1 we looked at the historical development of zero toler-ance expressed through the biographies of a group of early years practitioners. I concluded that zero tolerance had more to do with personal than professional perspectives. Do we perhaps project those personal perspectives inappropriately onto the more loud, active and sometimes aggressive behaviours of some little boys? At best, do we respond to their energy and exuberance as irritat-ingly alien and male? At worst, do we see them as wife beaters, armed robbers and rapists in the making? Do our sincere desires to eradicate violence cloud our ability to interpret their behaviour as play?

This last question relates back to the anxieties that many practi-tioners express in relation to the management of war, weapon and superhero play: they perceive it as aggression, and fear that it will lead to disruptive behaviour and real fighting. This issue of how practi-tioners perceive play fighting has been subject to a number of studies drawing on the work of Blurton-Jones (1967) who sought to apply an ethological approach to analysing children's play and identified a number of features used in subsequent studies to distinguish play fighting from real fighting and to analyse teacher perceptions in this area (Pellegrini 1988; Connor 1989; Costabile *et al.* 1991; Schafer and Smith 1996). These studies all suggest that teachers significantly over-estimate the proportion of pretend fighting which develops into real fighting, and Connor particularly concludes that the classification of aggressive behaviour is individually constructed and that the gender of the observer is a significant variable.

Schafer and Smith (1996), drawing on data across studies, conclude that something in the order of 1 per cent of pretend play develops into real aggression, rising to 25 per cent in children who are socially marginalized or with aggressive tendencies. This is considerably less than the teacher estimates (29 per cent in their sample).

In settings where zero tolerance has been relaxed many practitioners report that they are now more frequently standing back from play fighting events, which are a regular feature of war, weapon and superhero play, and have found that children are far more effective at managing play fighting themselves, both to avoid injury and to sustain the play, than they had previously believed possible. This has particularly been observed in episodes of sword fighting and superhero-karate style fight scenarios. In one setting I witnessed a boy and a girl assembling long lengths of plastic pipes to use in a sword fight. Instead of intervening I watched carefully. Before the game started they agreed that they had to be careful not to hit each other and that they had to stand quite a long way apart. After one child received a knock (nothing serious as the pipes were plastic) they decided that they needed to move further apart to prevent a repetition. They sustained the play with much posturing and laughter for 10–15 minutes until they decided they wanted to play elsewhere.

On other occasions in a number of settings I have seen children performing karate fights with such skill and precision that they resemble t'ai chi movements. I have seen less accidental kicking in settings where zero tolerance has been relaxed and I wonder if this is the result of children having the time and permission to practise these movements so that they have greater control. Clearly, suspending the assumption that play fighting inevitably leads to real fighting is an essential step for practitioners to take in reviewing both zero tolerance and their perceptions of this gendered play area.

Conclusion

In this chapter I have reviewed a number of current debates about, and perspectives on, the development of gender identity in early childhood. I have argued that the persistence of gender stereotyped behaviour among young children, after thirty years of anti-sexist, equal opportunities provision in early years settings, should not prompt despair and send us running back to biological explanations. Instead I have described ways in which common approaches to gender equity in early childhood settings may have served to reinforce these stereotyped behaviours, and have urged an honest and reflective review of practice in this area, which must encompass personal perspectives. I have stressed that current practices may be limiting the play and behaviour options for both girls and boys.

Zero tolerance has been highlighted as an approach which, although represented as being in the interests of gender equity, may in fact operate in a counter-productive way. Examples were given of both boys and girls crossing gender boundaries in settings where zero tolerance has been relaxed, demonstrating that this may well be a fertile area on which to focus in any review of gender work in early childhood.

3

THE POWER OF IMAGINATION

The concept of 'what might be' – being able to move in perception and thought away from the concrete given, or 'what is' to 'what was, what could have been, what one can try for, what might happen', and ultimately, to the purest realms of fantasy – is a touchstone of that miracle of human experience, the imagination.

(Singer and Singer 1990: 19)

In this chapter we shall be considering the importance of practitioners' understanding of children's imaginative development as it relates to war, weapon and superhero play.

In Chapter 1 I stated that war, weapon and superhero play should not be considered as separate and distinct from all other areas of play. This point will be addressed in this chapter by considering it as a form of imaginative play and by looking specifically at the ways in which a zero tolerance approach bars access to this important area of development for those boys with a persistent interest in such play themes. At the end of Chapter 2 we saw, for example, how relaxing zero tolerance impacted on the ability of children to cross gender boundaries in their exploration of role-play.

We will also look at how, by limiting access to these taboo play themes, we are perhaps inhibiting development which may serve to assist some of those young boys, at risk of becoming aggressive adults as a result of other social agendas present in their lives, from developing effective conflict resolution strategies which may mediate that risk.

The definition of imaginative play with which I shall be working is a broad one drawing on the opening quote from Singer and Singer (1990) and succinctly expressed by Bruce (1991: 59) in describing the features of 'free-flow play': 'It is about possible, alternative worlds, which involve "supposing" (Rubin *et al.* adapted), and "as if" (Atkins 1988).'

This exploration will encompass construction, small world play, role-play, socio-dramatic play and narrative. We will not be considering other areas of creative development like mark making in my discussions simply because it is not possible to cover everything in a single book, and I have selected the areas in which there is greatest evidence to draw on from my current data. Similarly the literature on the nature and value of imaginative play is extensive and I will not attempt to summarize it here, but do so in relation to my particular areas of interest throughout the chapter.

It may also be useful for me to summarize my own view of the role and importance of imagination in development, synthesized from a range of theoretical perspectives. Crucially, I view imagination as the thread that enables us to connect with other human minds. In Chapter 2 I referred to the perspective held by neuroscientists concerning the plasticity of the human brain and how experience will sculpt each individual's brain differently. It is this individuation in brain development that underpins the theory of mind (Lewis and Mitchell 1994) by which we come to understand that no other individual can precisely share our thoughts, memories and understanding of the world. Developing a theory of mind is one of the essential conceptual leaps that young children have to make in their early years: understanding that communication is not mind to mind despite the swift adult responses to their basic needs experienced by most, but sadly not all, children in their early days, weeks and months.

Vygotsky (1978: 93, 95) makes an interesting link between the increase in children's experience of delayed gratification and the onset of imaginative play. He suggests that this is not coincidental, as in imaginative play children are learning to subordinate their own needs by submitting to the rules developed within the play.

> However, at the preschool age, a great many unrealisable tendencies and desires emerge. It is my belief that if needs that could not be realized immediately did not develop during the school years, there would be no play, because play seems to be invented at the point when the child begins to experience unrealisable tendencies ... Whenever there is an imaginary situation in play, there are rules ...

Children are simultaneously developing an understanding of symbolic substitution by playing with objects in a transformatory way, which helps children to move from concrete to abstract thought, and experiencing themselves as more powerful and competent.

This aspect of development has been variously described by other writers in the field of early childhood (Bruner 1966; Bruce 1997a; Harris 2000), but perhaps most notably and resoundingly by Piaget and Inhelder (1969) through the concept of egocentric thought, which suggests that before the age of about 7 children are so bound by the concrete world that they cannot make the leap into abstract thinking which would allow them to see the world from another point of view.

Subsequent researchers (Donaldson 1978; Dunn 1988) have demonstrated that this ability to view a situation from different perspectives, to empathize or exercise a theory of mind, can develop much earlier in childhood. Central to the growth of this ability are both representation, in a general sense, and language as a specific element of this representational development.

The ability to view a situation from multiple perspectives, understanding that there are at least two sides to every story, is an essential element of effective conflict resolution, a view we espouse every time we bring children together after they have had a fight or dispute.

It might be argued that language is the primary medium through which theory of mind is established but, while it is clearly a central mechanism in this process, language, without the support of a rich bank of representations based on first-hand experiences and imagination, can never tell us all we need to know about the world and other minds. Language, however sophisticated, is just a conventional symbolic code (Bruner 1966) which allows us to share our thoughts, feelings and experiences in an approximate way with other human beings. Words spoken, or on a page, describing a landscape we have never visited, can only come alive in our heads if we can use our imaginations to make connections and project ourselves into possible worlds (Bruner 1986).

A curriculum for young children in which language is seen to lead cognitive development therefore runs the risk of marginalizing symbolic and imaginative play as a means by which children can come to an enriched understanding of language as a symbolic system allowing communication beyond the purely literal.

Vygotsky argues this point in relation to symbolic play and abstraction when he describes a child moving beyond the point where 'things dictate to the child what he must do' towards a point where 'thought is separated from objects and action arises from ideas rather from things: a piece of wood begins to be a doll and a stick becomes a horse' (Vygotsky 1978: 96). Thus a child involved in imaginative symbolic play learns that language, ideas and objects can be flexible. An object is not defined by its name and what it does; ideas can encompass what could be, as well as what is or what has been.

If the imagination is such a central mechanism in the realms of human communication, underpinning our ability both to comprehend and respect diversity and to conceive of change and growth in social contexts, then it surely follows that supporting such development should have a high priority for all those involved in working with young children. In writing about a new form of development theory, Bruner described this priority in the following words (1986: 149):

> It will be motivated by the question of how to create a new generation that can prevent the world from dissolving into chaos and destroying itself. I think that its central technical concern will be how to create in the young an appreciation of the fact that many worlds are possible, that meaning and reality are created and not discovered, that negotiation is the art of constructing new meanings by which individuals can regulate their relations with each other.

Many practitioners do not value war, weapon and superhero play as a form of imaginative play. Many feel that its themes are simply dictated by films, videos and TV series, which have limited and repetitive content based crudely on a struggle between good and evil and thus offer children little in terms of extended imaginative play. Moreover, children are re-enacting scenarios where force, often violent, wins out, which contradicts practitioners' efforts to resolve conflict peacefully. A major difficulty with this analysis is that because children are generally interrupted in such play scenarios I do not feel we can begin to evaluate the imaginative potential of such scenarios unless we allow them to develop.

It is also important to remember that children are not responsible for the media diet they are offered. That responsibility is one that rests entirely in the adult world. We have a choice, therefore, of either insisting that children leave such material at the nursery door, thus withholding support in helping them to deal with such material, or working with children to help them process and imaginatively transform such material.

Practitioners have also frequently commented that war, weapon and superhero play is more gratuitously violent now than it was historically as a result of this media influence, and the ubiquitous presence of guns is frequently cited in this discussion. I feel that there is a degree of romanticism behind this argument. The equivalent play theme when I was a child was cowboys and Indians. While the superior power of guns may have been a decisive factor in the real Indian wars, bows and arrows were as lethal as guns in the play battles waged by children. What makes such an intrinsically racist and brutal theme any more acceptable than the equally racist (the baddies are still nearly always represented as the dark force) but more high-tech version of the theme offered to young children today? The issue here is surely that as a society we need to engage far more actively in a struggle to influence the nature of media offered to young children to limit the more damaging oppressive undertones present in those texts. We must also remember that children are often exposed to media intended for an adult audience.

The other aspect of this discussion to consider is the appeal across time and place of the intrinsic struggle between good and evil that seems to hold such a powerful attraction for young children, particularly boys. The nature of the play which has emerged in settings where zero tolerance has been relaxed frequently starts from media reference points but over time these references are frequently effaced by the more central themes of childhood which seem to reside behind the packaging. Children themselves then seem to revert back to the more amorphous realm of ghosts, monsters and baddies whose attributes do not routinely reflect the racist or gendered stereotypes of their media diet.

The Othering of those different to oneself does not seem to reside so wholeheartedly at the centre of children's concerns as it does at the heart of those responsible for producing mainstream violence for children and adults. What seems, therefore, to be important for practitioners is to ensure, first, that by working with these themes we prevent the interpolation of the model of Otherness into their model of the world and, second, that violence does not become an overriding template for the resolution of conflict.

Many writers, particularly those rooted in a psychoanalytical tradition, have explored this apparently intrinsic need shown by children to explore the struggle between good and evil, goodies and baddies. Whatever view one holds about the psychoanalytical tradition I would suggest that the key arguments raised are important to consider, if only to prompt further reflective consideration of this persistent theme in children's play. Bettelheim is a useful source here and the following comment encapsulates the perspective I am introducing (Bettelheim 1978: 141):

Adults often think that the cruel punishment of an evil person in fairy tales upsets and scares children unnecessarily. Quite the opposite is true: such retribution reassures the child that the punishment fits the crime. The child often feels unjustly treated by adults and the world in general, and it seems that nothing is done about it. On the basis of such experiences alone, he wants those who cheat and degrade him . . . most severely punished . . . the more severely those bad ones are dealt with, the more secure the child feels.

The following three comments, made by practitioners in settings where zero tolerance has been relaxed, all focus on the development of imaginative play among boys with a persistent interest in war, weapon and superhero play. They suggest that war, weapon and superhero scenarios may in fact provide the seeds for imaginative development. The boys, whose chosen entry point to imaginative play had been effectively blocked and who had not been previously observed to involve themselves in alternative extended imaginative or representational play, were seen in a short period of time to flourish in these areas.

> The play became more creative, imaginative – it was interesting to see how they were using the equipment in the room and certain things would become something else . . . With this weapon play the aggression wasn't there towards each other . . . one child zapped another into another land rather than killing them.

> If we hadn't changed I don't think they would have moved on into what they have . . . Whereas before they would have just been shooting and running around mad, now they'll get into a really good role-play game and it will become part of it, but it's in the right context.

> We had quite a lot of children being quite aggressive, getting into fights, and we were wary that we would be encouraging that. But in fact we have seen amazing imaginative extended games develop, particularly outside. Children's games have not involved violence, just imagination running riot.

In future chapters we will examine more examples of the imaginative play which developed from these themes.

In addition we need to remember that we work with what the child brings to us. Practitioners routinely encounter a number of young boys for whom war, weapon and superhero play is their only play interest. For some of those boys zero tolerance means shutting the door and bolting it against their imaginative development. Some of them will be the children at risk of developing aggressive behaviour in the studies cited in Chapter 2.

Imagination and conflict resolution

In the ensuing section I will focus particularly on this evidence of the role of imaginative development in relation to conflict resolution strategies. I feel this is of particular relevance to the challenge I am proposing to zero tolerance of war, weapon and superhero play as an effective means of intervening in the spiral of male violence. I will summarize a number of research perspectives on this issue as I wish to show that they coalesce to stress the significance of the role of imaginative development in the inhibition of aggressive behaviours.

One of the common responses I have heard made initially by practitioners at workshops in relation to my action research is, 'Yes, we should let them get it out of their systems; they need to act it out in their play.' This draws heavily on a received understanding of Freud's cathartic drive reduction theory:

> Catharsis theory further stipulates that when the individual engages in fantasized aggression, small quantities of energy are discharged, thus reducing the pressure of the aggressive drive.
>
> (Biblow 1973: 105)

Because of the populist recourse to this view I believe it is important to raise and challenge it here, as it perhaps limits our understanding of the more far-ranging role that fantasy and imagination have to play in relation to conflict resolution. While Biblow (1973) asserts the importance of fantasy in reducing displays of real aggression, he challenges the orthodox Freudian view of this cathartic mechanism, which supposes that aggressive fantasies can reduce the need to act on aggressive feelings. Building on earlier research, which suggests that it is only highly imaginative children who can draw on aggressive or non-aggressive fantasy material to reduce their own aggressive responses (Biblow 1973: 107–9), he conducted a study with a group of 9 to 10-year-old children of both high- and low-fantasy disposition, to examine the use they made of aggressive and non-aggressive fantasy material to control their responses to frustration. This study confirmed his hypothesis that

> While catharsis theory maintains that aggression is hydraulically drained away or purged from the individual through a

quantitative lessening of his aggressive drive, it is hypothesized that the high-fantasy individual uses fantasy to change his prevailing affective state or mood from an angry one to a new and distinct mood.

(Biblow 1973: 109)

There are three major implications of this research that seem pertinent to the argument I am formulating. The first is that it raises a challenge to a laissez-faire attitude to war, weapon and superhero play as a means of burning off aggressive energy which could be concluded from my research findings and which I would not wish to promulgate. This view is contained in such comments as, 'It's just a phase they go through', 'They need to run around and burn off their anger.'

The second concerns the fact that Biblow's study was conducted with a group of children older than those being considered in my research. The findings suggest that to avoid the differences noted between high- and low-fantasy subjects at 9 and 10 the development of children's imaginative capacities in the early years is crucial. Therefore, we need to engage with children's war, weapon and superhero play in order to maximize the imaginative development of children involved in it.

The third implication is that children whose imaginative functioning is underdeveloped would not be able to utilize fantasy as a means of controlling aggressive feelings and might be more likely to act on them (Biblow 1973: 127). This matches with observations made at my research settings that children who had been more prone to actual aggression during zero tolerance were less frequently involved in such behaviour when this approach was relaxed and they had been observed to become involved in extended imaginative play. Locking children out of imaginative play by operating a ban on their chosen fantasy material would seem, in relation to Biblow's research, to prevent them from acquiring skills which could reduce their involvement in real aggressive behaviour.

Another perspective is offered in a piece of research which focuses on the relationship between imagination and reasoning in 4 to 5-year-old children (Dias and Harris 1990). They are concerned with facilitating young children's ability to reason against 'empirical bias' (Dias and Harris 1990: 305); for example, if told that Barny is a dog and that all dogs moo, they would not draw the conclusion that Barny would moo, because their experience of dogs has already taught them that this would not be the case (Dias and Harris 1990: 317). Such reasoning is clearly implicated in the ability to hypothesize, which underpins the problem-solving approaches to learning we seek to foster in the early years.

This ability would also seem to be of specific importance in relation to conflict resolution aspirations by enabling children to rewrite aggressive media scripts, their possible lived experiences of violence, conflict and retaliation, or stereotyped gender roles. It is interesting to note that much of the media material which causes us concern, such as Power Rangers, depends on characters acting against children's 'empirical bias' by committing impossible acts of transformation. It is possible that we could use such material in supporting the development of the skills of reasoning highlighted in the above research. Dias and Harris (1990: 312) found that children were able to use these 'systematic reasoning' skills in imaginative contexts:

> The presence of any of the three cues – imagery, a reference to a different setting or a make believe intonation – markedly improved children's accuracy in reasoning from premises that violated their real world knowledge.

Clearly, sound imaginative functioning is again highlighted as essential in underpinning an ability which could support children in resolving conflict and avoiding aggressive behaviour. As Dias and Harris (1990: 317) state: 'It is clear that the child's imagination is much more than a device for escaping from present reality or for reproducing some past experience.'

Support for the relationship between well-developed imaginative functioning and low levels of aggressive behaviour are also supported by Singer's longitudinal observational research into this connection (1994: 12):

> Our research studies of 3–4 year old children followed for 1 year indicate that those who played more often at make believe or who developed imaginary playmates were also reported by observers to be more likely to smile and laugh during the play school situation, be more persistent and less likely to be angry, aggressive or sad. In studies of imaginative older children we find them to be less unwarrantedly aggressive, less impulsive and better able to discriminate reality from fantasy.

A more recent study by Judy Dunn and Claire Hughes (2001) of the fantasy play themes used by 40 hard-to-manage and 40 control children at 4 found, when the children were followed up at age 6, that those children with an interest in violent play themes demonstrated less socially developed behaviour including their ability to show empathy. The results also showed that 'the children whose pretend play included a high proportion of violent fantasies were less frequently engaged in pretence than the children whose fantasies were not violent' (Dunn and Hughes 2001: 502).

My inference from these studies is not a causal connection between violent fantasy play and aggressive behaviour but rather that imaginative development through fantasy play may be implicated in successful social development and conflict resolution. While I would not contend from my own evidence that all children with a persistent interest in war, weapon and superhero play are at risk from other social agendas, a number are, and it would seem pertinent, therefore, to consider working with these play interests in order to promote imaginative development rather than against them by enforcing zero tolerance.

Taming the amygdala

Finally, I wish to consider a perspective which, although it does not directly address the impact of imagination on the management of aggressive behaviour, implies it through an explanation of the neuro-physiology of this process. Daniel Goleman (1996: 13–29) describes the tension between the amygdala, the area of the brain which stores emotional memory, and the neocortical area, which acts as a control mechanism to the more impulsive, reflex-orientated responses of the amygdala. The amygdala, except in an alarming or threatening situation, would generally be activated by the more circumspect neocortical area. He outlines a process, 'neural hijacking' (p. 26), whereby the amygdala, fired by input that has bypassed the neocortical area, 'can react in a delirium of rage or fear before the cortex knows what is going on because such raw emotion is triggered independent of, and prior to, thought'. While such responses have their uses in fight or flight situations they are clearly less helpful in day-to-day situations, and may account for such a phenomenon as road rage.

Goleman suggests that 'emotional intelligence' (1996), which can maintain the balance between amygdala and neocortex, thus avoiding neural hijacking, can be developed and describes some programmes in schools aimed at doing so. While he does not cite imaginative play as being pertinent to this development his descriptions of emotionally intelligent responses, which circumvent neural hijacking, suggest an ability to visualize alternative scenarios, as also indicated in the examples of research into imaginative play cited above. The following description outlines this sort of response:

> Say someone in another car cuts dangerously close to you as you are driving on the freeway. If your reflexive thought is 'That son

of a bitch!' it matters immensely for the trajectory of rage whether that thought is followed by more thoughts of outrage and revenge . . . Contrast that sequence of building rage with a more charitable line of thought toward the driver who cut you off: 'Maybe he didn't see me, or maybe he had some good reason for driving so carelessly, such as a medical emergency.' That line of possibility tempers anger with mercy, or at least an open mind, short-circuiting the buildup of rage.

(Goleman 1996: 59)

This example calls to mind the children described in Pellegrini's (1988) study referred to in Chapter 2 who were not regarded as popular, frequently misunderstood behavioural cues, responded aggressively to playful gestures and accidental bumps and who were far more likely to be involved in play fights escalating into real fights than popular children. It seems possible that these children might be displaying signs of 'neural hijacking'. It would appear that the flourishing of imaginative play in the young boys previously frozen out by zero tolerance, if nurtured, may in fact be harnessed to serve their future as non-aggressive adults, which raises further challenges to assumptions about war, weapon and superhero play feeding future aggression.

Alongside the enhanced imaginative development of some boys with a persistent interest in this area of play noted earlier in this chapter, additional benefits to their social development have been observed. Allowing them to pursue their play interests has given them a means to make friends through sharing skills in constructing weapons or knowledge of particular TV programmes or characters.

Darren's story

To illustrate the interplay of these benefits I would like to tell you the story of one child I encountered during my research. His name is Darren, and when I first met him in the nursery class of an inner London primary school he fitted Pellegrini's (1988) description of the socially rejected child. He was also obsessed with gun play. His first act on arrival at nursery would be to head for whatever construction materials were available, make a gun and attempt to play with it. Daily his attempts to play would be frustrated, perhaps exacerbating his existing difficulties at making and sustaining friendships. He routinely hit out at other children, isolating himself still further.

The team were in the process of referring Darren through the special needs assessment framework because of their concerns about his behaviour. They came to discover that he had a history of glue ear and associated hearing difficulties which helped to make sense of his emotional and learning delays. Simultaneously the nursery coordinator, following attendance at a workshop I had run, decided that relaxing zero tolerance might help Darren to extricate himself from the corner that he had metaphorically been backed into. Constantly saying 'no' to a child lacking in broader play interests and experiences and with little self-esteem was clearly not a helpful strategy.

After zero tolerance was relaxed Darren was legitimately able to pursue his interests. He had time to develop his construction skills and other children admired his prowess at making guns, seeking his help and advice. He began routinely to make two guns each morning: one for himself and one for a friend. Initially his play was largely of the 'bang, bang you're dead' variety but his repertoire developed to incorporate more sophisticated chasing, hiding and ambushing sequences. Sometimes other children would be the baddies but more often than not his opponents would be imaginary.

His group of friends increased and their often more sophisticated imaginative play skills influenced and broadened his skills. He became popular and, although he would still sometimes push or hit out these incidents became less frequent and were more readily resolved: he learned to say sorry and hug a child to make him or her feel better. These incidents did not generally arise directly from the play scenario. The hitting was real; the gun play was fantasy. Was imaginative development perhaps supporting his ability to empathize or was it a combination of that alongside his actual experience of relating closely to others that the imaginative play fostered? The question cannot be definitively answered, but he was clearly benefiting in multiple ways from the relaxation of zero tolerance.

After seven to eight months his imaginative play began to flourish in more extended ways. Darren was observed concealing guns in bags from the home corner with a friend and heading off on a journey. Shortly afterwards he was seen transforming his guns into electric paddles as seen in TV hospital series to revive children who had been shot in the game. This theme expanded over the coming weeks so that Darren became Dr Darren, with further acts of imaginative transformation being observed. On one occasion I watched him constructing aeroplanes after he had observed two other children doing so. I had only ever seen him making a gun from construction materials previously and the electric paddles started life as a brace of pistols.

On my last visit, just before Darren moved on to the reception class, I witnessed Dr Darren, while he was being pushed in a wooden buggy to revive his next patient, break up his omnipresent gun and transform it into a plate of food to eat on his journey.

Darren continued to make guns but far less frequently. When I subsequently visited him in his reception class I watched him spend an outdoor play session engrossed in sand play. His teacher reported that gun play was infrequent and that Darren was making good progress in all areas and was interested in a range of activities.

The act of transformation I have described above, when Darren turned his gun into food, reminiscent of the biblical notion of turning swords into ploughshares, leads me into a brief discussion of the difference between manufactured toy guns and weapons made from construction kits or found materials.

I think a major distinction is to be drawn and I would never advocate that manufactured weapons should be brought into early years settings. The distinction rests on this possibility of transformation. A manufactured weapon is a single purpose toy and directs the child in how to play with it. A toy gun is to be pointed and shot and indeed there is not a lot else that can be done with it. The toy determines the play, not the child. Constructing a weapon, however, involves an initial act of imagination and transformation and, as we have seen from Darren's example, one such act can lead to others.

So, does the imaginative development that I have been describing occur spontaneously when zero tolerance is relaxed? In some cases, where a setting is already offering a rich imaginative curriculum and the children concerned have already achieved a reasonable level of imaginative functioning, the answer to this question is yes. However, experience across a number of settings suggests that some practitioners and some children need help in developing the skills necessary to support effective imaginative play. This is an area of challenge for many practitioners because they may lack confidence in supporting imaginative play generally or may feel specifically alienated by the particular scenarios related to war, weapon and superhero play, or perhaps because they feel that it is de facto wrong ever to intervene in children's imaginative play. Setting managers have corroborated this in case study interviews by stating that after relaxing zero tolerance imaginative play has flourished under the influence of particular practitioners who are confident both about planning responsively for imaginative play and about spontaneous involvement with children's imaginative play when appropriate.

My own observations similarly suggest that where practitioners are most anxious about their ability to support and extend war, weapon and superhero play they have generally given less active support to imaginative play, particularly outside and particularly for boys. The issue then seems to be less about war, weapon and superhero play in particular and more about imaginative play in general. In later chapters we will examine examples of good practice in this area.

I would suggest that the key reasons for this difficulty lie partially in the fact that imaginative development is not necessarily a high priority in early childhood training. I also feel that, historically, distorted interpretations of Piaget, emphasizing the preparation of the environment and minimal intervention and ignoring his concern with adult interaction, have outweighed the more explicitly social interactionist perspectives of Vygotsky and Bruner.

While in general I support caution in relation to the over-involvement of adults and the over-direction of children's play, I do not believe that this should result in a laissez-faire approach. As we have seen from many of the research studies cited in this chapter, not all children enter our settings with an equal facility in imaginative play. We need to be able to recognize those children and to act appropriately to support them while not casting an adult shadow over play that is 'free-flowing' (Bruce 1991, 1997a).

This may involve work behind the scenes in terms of resourcing to facilitate imaginative play and it might also require more direct support in the form of play partnerships between adults and children to model imaginative scenarios and to increase children's imaginative play vocabularies. Some settings have followed up on their work with me around war, weapon and superhero play with an in-service training programme for the team around supporting imaginative play in general. The role of the adult must not be underestimated.

> Memories of pretend play are often associated with a special person who encouraged play, told fantastic stories, or modelled play by initiating games, who perhaps had a flamboyant personality that inspired imitation or gave wonderful gifts of puppets and picture books or shared exotic travel adventures – who, above all, showed a trusting, loving acceptance of children and their capacity for playfulness.
>
> (Singer and Singer 1990: 4)

To conclude, I believe that, in order for practitioners to support successfully the imaginative development of children from the springboard of war, weapon and superhero play, they may first need to extend the imaginative landscape inside themselves to refresh that sense of possible worlds that we wish to bring to children. We need to look beyond the weapon to see the child holding it.

4

RELAXING ZERO TOLERANCE: THE EXPERIENCE OF ONE SETTING

In the first three chapters we examined a range of theoretical challenges to a zero tolerance approach. The debates and concerns that we explored there will now be reviewed through a description and analysis of the experience of children and practitioners in one inner London under-fives centre when we decided to relax our zero tolerance approach to war, weapon and superhero play. The centre is a 64-place local authority centre offering full-time places to children from the age of 2 to 5. Children who attend the centre represent the rich diversity of the local community in terms of class, cultural and linguistic backgrounds. We will consider the positive impact on the quality of role-play and the extension of play choices for boys with a dominant interest in war, weapon and superhero play. We will also look at the impact of the change on the perceptions of practitioners and on the 'genderscape' of classrooms in the setting.

The background

Zero tolerance had been in place in the centre for as long as anyone working there could remember. The longest serving member of the team of ten had worked there for fifteen years. We looked at the variety in the personal and professional trajectories that led the members of the team to support this approach in Chapter 1, but we need to remind ourselves of them here.

Some members of the team had a clear personal agenda influenced by the peace and women's liberation movements, which led them to believe that zero tolerance was an approach of early intervention consistent with their desire to break the spiral of male domestic and military aggression. Other members of the team had encountered zero tolerance during their training or first jobs and felt that it made common sense to discourage children from engaging with play that they felt to be aggressive. The third group of practitioners felt that they had simply been following policy and had not questioned the reasons for this approach. Zero tolerance was consistently and vigorously applied across the setting.

Children who constructed weapons or started enacting war or superhero scenarios would be interrupted, reminded of the rules and the reasons for them, and encouraged to engage with other activities. Sometimes children would be asked to break up a weapon they had made. Children would even be cut short in a group discussion if they tried to introduce ideas or experiences related to fighting or weapons. I have to own that I was one of the most vigorous 'enforcers' within the team.

Before moving on to look in detail at the effects of our change in approach it may be helpful to dwell for a while on the motivation for that change. Theoretical support for those changes has been considered already, but the original act of change was inspired by real dilemmas in practice and the impact of a zero tolerance approach on real children.

Why we changed

The story begins in one of the two nursery classes in the centre. In that particular group of 26 children there were typically three boys with a consuming interest in war, weapon and superhero play – Fred, Magnus and Jon. Others would more occasionally show an interest in these taboo themes but Fred, Magnus and Jon would attempt to pursue this play on a daily basis and would have their attempts rebuffed several times during each of those days.

They were not readily distracted from their interests and would rarely become absorbed in other activities for sustained periods of time. They were restless, frequently involved in aggressive incidents with each other and other children and thus were the frequent recipients of reprimands from all members of the team.

Magnus and Jon had a strong friendship and were lost when the other was absent, clearly finding it difficult to form other relationships. Fred was desperate to form a bond with Jon and was frequently excluded by the pair. He had an extended day place (from 8am to 5.30pm) at the centre and although he connected with other children in that particular group at the beginning and end of the day these relationships did not seem to sustain him in the nursery class context.

The three boys were seen as being noisy, aggressive and distracting to the other children, and thus having a negative impact on the dynamics of the class.

Concerns about their disruptive behaviour and failure to settle down to activities that we saw as cognitively beneficial were frequently expressed to their parents/carers. These discussions would include our concerns about their preoccupation with war, weapon and superhero play and requests to discourage them from this inappropriate behaviour. We were concerned that these children were not gaining access to the range of learning experiences on offer, and about the impact of this on their imaginative and cognitive development. It would be fair to say that we regarded these boys as challenging and that we felt their problems resided in their home experiences. We had not been making any connection with our business-as-usual zero tolerance approach to their play interests.

The centre, however, has an established ethos of concern for individual children's well-being, with a framework of routine weekly team meetings to review children's progress and a high management expectation of observation and monitoring of all children. The centre had only recently come under the wing of the local education authority, having been previously managed by social services, and the centre management and staff team had ensured that the care element of the centre's ethos had not been lost in the move to the education authority.

As a practitioner whose previous experience had been in the school sector I learnt much in this area from the accumulated wisdom of the centre team. While the behaviour of the three boys was of concern, and while we were barking up the wrong tree in our hunt for a solution, there was a central concern and determination shown by the team to understand the boys' behaviour and to find appropriate strategies to deal with it. We were thus involved in a constant process of review.

We had already identified the spiral of negative attention as being an issue of concern with these children and had trialled a strategy of allocating one member of the team to start the day by participating with them in whatever activity they might choose on arrival. The idea was to begin the day with positive interactions and to steer their actions into appropriate areas. If, for example, they headed to the construction carpet the allocated adult would join them and try to deflect them from making weapons by suggesting and modelling alternatives. The strategy enjoyed some success as the boys welcomed the adult participation, positive interest and interactions. They would generally be happy and settled for this initial part of the day and were willing to build vehicles and castles, but after the adult had withdrawn the play and behaviour returned to the previous patterns.

The partial success of this strategy allowed us to see that these children could and would respond to positive adult interactions. This, coupled with the increasingly focused observations of some of the team members of the crestfallen responses of these boys to our constant hijacking of their play and rejection of their constructions, led us to look more closely at their well-being. Our focus changed from looking at external causes for their behaviour to considering the impact of our own practice. This relates back to the analysis in Chapter 2 of Fred's experience of zero tolerance. We started to try to view our practice through the boys' eyes and became increasingly aware of how blinkered our perceptions of their behaviour had become.

We had become so preoccupied with the disruptive elements of their conduct that we had failed to see that they were unhappy; they rarely smiled or laughed; they lacked confidence and self-esteem; their responses to our offers of alternative activities were not neutral, they were often overlaid with anxiety ('I can't do that'), nor were they popular or part of an extended friendship network. In concert with these realizations I had started to read material from the American context questioning a zero tolerance approach (Carlsson-Paige and Levin 1990). The stage was set for a radical change.

We were embarking on a process that involved 'a personal confronting and reconstruction rather than an application of another's thinking . . .' (Francis 1997: 171).

What we did

The possibility of relaxing zero tolerance was first discussed in the room team and then with the whole centre team. Despite the strong feelings held by many members of the team in support of zero tolerance, it was generally agreed that the approach was not working in any case because we were consistently having to expend a lot of energy in policing it; they shared concern about the particular impact on the three boys, and some had a strong sense of discomfort with constantly saying 'no' to young children. Although our concerns at the time centred on particular children, it was generally acknowledged that such a group existed in practically every intake and that the problems we were encountering were not new. All members of the team agreed to suspend their personal agendas and to bring to the fore their professional commitment to developing policies that were in the best interests of the children.

Here we draw on Dewey's (1933) notion of a community of inquiry marked by 'open mindedness', which recognises the possibilities raised in others' perspectives, 'responsibility' for considering the ethical and moral dimensions of the choices we make as teachers and the 'wholeheartedness' with which we attempt to identify and examine the limitations in our assumptions and world views.

(Francis 1997: 172)

We agreed to relax zero tolerance initially for half a term in order to see how the play would develop and whether this would have any beneficial effects on the particular children that we had concerns about. Children would be allowed to construct weapons and to point or shoot them at ceiling, sky, walls, ground or imaginary enemies, but not at people. This boundary was set because we felt it would help children to keep issues of real violence in mind and would maintain a border between fantasy and reality. We also felt it would help to limit the number of other children being intimidated by those involved in aggressive scenarios.

To some extent this boundary was equally a reflection of our own anxieties about letting go of zero tolerance. Most of us found it particularly difficult to see children pointing guns at each other and this boundary would allow us to retain some control. The rationale for this boundary can be readily challenged as being inconsistent in that on the one hand we were allowing gun play as an act of imaginative play while on the other controlling the imaginative scope or framework of that play.

I would not defend this boundary in an absolute way, but any policy is only as effective as the practitioners who apply it and, especially given the innovative and risky step we were taking, the new approach had to be sustainable by that particular team. It was as far as we felt able to go at that point. I think it was a successful strategy insofar as it provided the team with a transitional situation that allowed us to become more confident with the emerging play without personal boundaries being transgressed too frequently. This boundary has been a subject of extensive debate among practitioners and will be reviewed in greater depth in Chapter 5.

The team also agreed that it was essential to ensure that the overall behaviour policy was clearly applied to war, weapon and superhero play. We were concerned that no child should feel intimidated or have their play disrupted by active, noisy and possibly aggressive play scenarios and we were equally clear that zero tolerance should still apply to any incidents of real aggression and fighting. We hoped that by effectively applying the behaviour policy we could separate the play forms from negative behaviour. We needed to feel clear that in relinquishing one boundary we were not abandoning them all. This issue also formed an important element in our discussions with parents/carers, which preceded our change of approach.

All parents received a letter detailing the proposed change, which emphasized our reasons for making the change and that the behaviour policy would be upheld. We explained that careful observation and monitoring would be taking place and that a review would be made after a term before deciding on ongoing policy. Parents/carers were invited to comment and key workers followed up on the letter by speaking individually to all parents/carers. Opportunities for discussion were also provided when we circulated letters seeking permission for the video observations we wished to make of the play that would arise from the point where we would have previously intervened.

Despite our anxieties about parental responses only one parent objected strongly to the proposed change, which she withdrew after extensive reassurance that the behaviour policy would be stringently upheld. The parents of the boys with a persistent interest were all extremely relieved by our proposals. They had been made to feel, not just by us but also in the broader context of friends and family, that their sons were badly adjusted, problem children and that they were 'bad' or inadequate parents. The changes we were proposing made them feel that a more open discussion about their children, their play interests and development could now be held. They felt supported rather than attacked. Anxieties about parental responses have been an issue for many practitioners in settings changing policy and there will be more discussion of this issue in Chapter 5.

During discussions about how we would implement the change of approach we had decided against introducing the idea to the children en masse as we felt this might have the effect of prompting the play and we wished the process to be more organic. We decided to discuss the change and the agreed boundaries as play incidents arose. Again, approaches to this have varied between settings and these will be discussed later in the book. One of the lessons we learned from children's responses was the extent to which they had been aware of our prescriptive approach and therefore the level of challenge and resistant behaviour that was embedded in their persistence in playing war, weapon and superhero scenarios.

What happened

In the first days of the changed approach children would be waiting for us to challenge them when they were 'caught' making a gun or staging a Power Rangers fight. On these occasions we would explain that we had realized how much they liked to play in this way and that we were going to let them do so as long as they didn't shoot at other children and adults and that they didn't frighten, hurt or disturb anyone. The rule about shooting at other people was readily accepted and children were soon heard to remind each other about it if the boundary was crossed. I suspect that children were so surprised and relieved by the lifting of the outright ban that it didn't occur to them to protest about the limitations being imposed. Some of their initial reactions are recorded in Table 4.1.

The general impact on children's play was described by all members of the team, in interviews reflecting on the process, as having two stages. Initially there was a significant increase in the volume of war, weapon and superhero play and this included a number of children who had not previously been seen to have a particular interest. It is impossible to know if this was contagion, an indication of the number of children who played out these scenarios at home but followed the settings rules to the letter, or a combination of both factors.

Whatever the reasons, the first three to four weeks of the changeover were challenging for all concerned. Noise levels and the amount of physical play spiralled and the situation, particularly outside, sometimes felt chaotic. Because we were not used to some of the play forms burgeoning around us, and because part of our intention was to reduce the number of times we were saying no to children, we also found it initially challenging to use our behaviour policy effectively and to establish boundaries. It would be fair to say that we were initially overwhelmed, but we were also determined to keep our nerve, as we knew that any change of this scale would take time to settle down. And settle down it did. Table 4.1 summarizes these two phases of change in the words of the practitioners involved.

A significant element of this data that we need to note is that, while three practitioners only chose to record that war play had declined after the initial surge, the remaining seven noted that there had been major subsequent changes in some children's play. Five of these seven describe war play as now occurring 'in context' and the overall impression given is one of more extended role-play sequences.

These observations seem to support the idea discussed in Chapter 3 that zero tolerance may inhibit the development of the imaginative play of those children preoccupied with war, weapon and superhero play. It is also important to note that only one practitioner, when commenting on short-term changes, suggests that there was any increase in overall aggression. Three practitioners highlight that in the long term they felt that aggression and aggressive play had

Table 4.1 Responses to interview question 'What changes in children's play did you notice when we lifted our total ban on war, weapon and superhero play?'

Initial	Subsequent
Everything was a gun or sword – mostly guns – felt uncontrollable as if we'd let them loose – perhaps because they had the choice to do it all the time they thought 'let's go mad' – and they were spiteful, aggressive.	It carried on with 4–5 children – some dropped it, some carried on, certain children carried on.
Went through a phase of doing it a lot because it was now something they were allowed to do. At first it was like 'come on, let's do it, because either she's gone mad or she's made a mistake'.	Then because they knew they could do it and it was part of their overall play, they didn't do it as much. Once they realized it was going to carry on it fizzled out.
At first there was a lot of gun making.	It calmed down after a while – new children coming in stirred it up again.
There were lots of weapons made initially.	Now it's less but they are play-acting in meaningful contexts with what they've made instead of being sneaky. There is less straight violence.
Before it got better it got worse.	If we hadn't changed I don't think they would have moved on into what they have, and they still do it, but with purpose – it's always part of the game rather than the whole thing. Whereas before they would have just been shooting and running around mad, now they'll get into a really good role-play game and it will become part of it, but it's in the right context.

Continued

Table 4.1 *continued.*

Initial	Subsequent
Children were shocked – there was lots of eye contact to see if we'd stop them – eventually they got used to it.	Now gun play has dropped off and they are doing things they wouldn't have done before. The attention seeking stuff has stopped. When it happens now it is in context with a purpose – not the whole game.
At first confusion – why am I not getting usual attention?	Then play changed quite dramatically. The play became more creative, imaginative – it was interesting to see how they were using equipment in the room and certain things would become something else. For example, drumbeaters would become arrows, long tubes would become swords. With this weapon play the aggression wasn't there towards each other – for example in the garden instead of zapping each other in an aggressive manner one child zapped another into another land rather than killing them. Some girls started getting involved.
A lot initially.	Weapon play has actually died down and when it is being used it is in context – they are actually playing a game. Now the gun could be a laser, taking me to another country or changing me into something. It's a lot more in context rather than the violent aspect. I think it has boosted certain children's learning development because I've seen shifts. One child is a lot more confident. He will try other activities that he didn't really want to do before, and with two other children there's less of that chasing each other with intent to harm – there's more of them working in partnership, they're actually playing together.

actually diminished. Practitioners in other settings have corroborated this experience. As one deputy, Sheila Harrison, noted (2000: 11)

> We had quite a lot of children being quite aggressive, getting into fights, and we were wary that we would be encouraging that. But, in fact, we have seen amazing imaginative extended games develop, particularly outside. Children's games have not involved violence, just imagination running riot.

No settings have reported an escalation in real aggression over time although many feel overwhelmed by the initial increase in aggressive play and language.

The period of transition noted in the comments in Table 4.1 lasted for approximately three to four weeks. Other settings have experienced a longer transitional period and in one particular setting play continued on this transitional plateau for several months. Possible reasons for these differences will be explored in Chapter 6 but as a general comment I would suggest that they rest chiefly with the level of support given to the emerging play. In the context under discussion here it was not only the play which changed over the transitional period but also practitioners' perceptions of the play and their actions towards it. I would suggest that these changes were intrinsically linked to each other.

Developing the play

During this period practitioners became more confident about separating the toys and play from the behaviours and confidently applying the behaviour policy in relation to the play. Subsequently practitioners were able to begin to read and analyse their observations of the play through the analytical frameworks they applied to other forms of play. Consequently they began to plan for the play, noting individual children's particular interests, and to resource activities more appropriately. This included extending the stock of dressing-up clothes and making them available outside the home corner so that they were more widely accessible to children, particularly those boys who rarely ventured in there. This allowed a number of boys to elaborate on the roles they were playing and to explore, however germinally, ideas of characterization.

Support was also given for prop making in the technology area so that swords and fighter planes could be made at the woodwork bench. Thought was given to the range and shapes of the materials made available, for example tubes, paper cups and cones, in order to facilitate the particular representations related to war, weapon and superhero play.

Adult involvement also extended into more direct intervention in children's role-play, as discussed on a theoretical level at the end of Chapter 2. This intervention occurred on occasions when children's play appeared to be stuck in that they could not move beyond posturing with costumes and props, or extend an opening scenario. Care was always taken not to intervene in 'free-flowing' (Bruce 1991: 60) sequences of play and to ensure that the children welcomed the presence of the adult. One such intervention is described below (Holland 1999a: 4):

> Their Batman scenario consisted chiefly of jumping in and out of a Batmobile, constructed from hollow blocks, and running from one area of the room to another striking combative poses. On one particularly stressful morning noise levels were rising and the cry of 'Don't run inside please', was being repeated to no avail and with an increasingly menacing edge. At this point I decided to jump on the Batmobile at its next stop to see if I could usefully reroute it.
>
> I was welcomed wholeheartedly into the game, a reception I would not necessarily expect if children were absorbed in free-flow dramatic play, and my suggestion that we go hunting for the 'flat monsters' I'd heard were hiding under the sofa was received with relish. I hinted that surprise was of the essence and this resulted in four boys crawling and slithering silently across the room to peer under the sofa. When I mentioned that guns might be of no use, but that water might 'melt' the monsters, I was not mocked. Imaginary water containers were fetched from the Batmobile and water was poured and squirted under the sofa. The boys embraced the scenario: some got nasty flat monster bites and needed urgent treatment. Others spotted the monsters escaping and trying to steal the Batmobile.
>
> The group increased to six to eight children, including three girls, which I thought was reminiscent of the flood of girls to the construction carpet when a female worker gets down and works there. The play continued for 25 minutes. On another Batmobile journey I rode pillion behind two boys. The driver, a boy from the previous group, declared as we set off on a monster hunt, that the child sitting between us was sick. The Batmobile journey transformed into a drama of casualty waiting rooms, beds, pillows, blankets and t.l.c., all relevant and real recent experiences for him. I was able to withdraw once we got to the casualty waiting room, because he was so clearly in charge of his

play. This episode at least gives me hope that he can now see that the Batmobile is not pre-programmed; it can take him wherever he wants to go.

The most significant overall support to children's war, weapon and superhero play was probably the day-to-day validation of children's interests and creative endeavours. This meant, for example, that Fred, Magnus and Jon started to receive praise and acknowledgement for the weapons or superhero vehicles that they constructed. This acknowledgement would be largely focused on the effort and construction features. Practitioners might explore ideas of the difference between real and pretend weapons and the child might be asked to describe particular features of their construction. This often revealed unexpected responses as in the comment noted in Table 4.1 about the weapon that zapped people to a different country. Ideas that had previously been locked inside children's heads by the force of taboo were revealed and could be built on, not just through adult intervention and suggestion but also through peer group interaction. Practitioners were, in a nutshell, 'tuning in to children' (Bruce 1996).

By legitimizing and engaging with the play in these various ways we were able both to challenge our own negative assumptions about where the play would lead, i.e. that play fighting would inevitably lead to real aggression (Pellegrini 1988; Connor 1989) and to extend the play itself. We were able to

[introduce] shades of grey to the polarised media construct of good and bad ... model negotiation, prison or magic spells rather than violent death as punishment, and ... challenge racist (good/white, bad/black) and helpless female stereotypes. In doing this we open the doors to other possible fantasy realms.
(Holland 1999a: 5)

And the girls?

In Table 4.1 one practitioner referred to the increased involvement of girls in war, weapon and superhero play and I noted in the Batmobile sequence their participation in related dramatic play sequences when an adult was participating. Their participation in these scenarios was active and enthusiastic and girls often revealed a high level of knowledge about the characters and themes being drawn on, which gives the lie to the assumption that girls are simply not interested in this area of play.

After the experience of adult participation and thus approval of the play a number of girls did choose independently to join in with superhero themed play, although they were rarely seen to initiate it. Interestingly, girls were rarely seen to show an interest in weapon construction: their interest seemed to rest more squarely with the chase and vanquishing of foes themes underlying much of the dramatic play that emerged. As noted by Pellegrini and Smith (1998), this is one area of physical activity play in which gender differences are less marked, that is to say that girls are more significantly represented in this area.

Overall it was observed that there was an increase in the number of gender-mixed play groups across a range of activities, not just in specific war, weapon and superhero-related play. This may be a reflection of the loosening of some of the gender boundaries discussed in Chapter 2 as adults were seen to chastise boys' more noisy and active play less frequently, thus facilitating a greater possibility of border crossing. It became possible to be a girl and play in a noisy and active way. It became possible to be a boy and play with girls because there was a common play interest.

Benefits to individual children

To conclude this chapter I will return to Fred, Magnus and Jon to consider the particular impact that the changes had on them. The three children are those referred to by the following comment in Table 4.1:

> If we hadn't changed I don't think they would have moved on into what they have, and they still do it, but with purpose – it's always part of the game rather than the whole thing. Whereas before they would have just been shooting and running around mad, now they'll get into a really good role-play game and it will become part of it, but it's in the right context.

Perhaps because the play was legitimized and became a more open forum the social barriers that had previously existed seemed to soften and playgroups became larger, more fluid and more inclusive. This may be because of the familiarity and relative simplicity of the play themes that allowed children to join the play readily. Fred, with his expertise in weapon construction and superhero themes, became a popular playmate for both Magnus and Jon and other children in the centre. Instead of his daily diet of negative responses he was receiving regular praise for his construction efforts, prop making and dressing up as his favourite superhero characters.

In addition he was receiving focused adult attention within his role-play to extend themes and story lines. This allowed him to become more independent in his play and facilitated a deeper level of involvement and enhanced well-being (Laevers *et al.* 1997). Magnus and Jon required less support in their play, but the relaxing of zero tolerance enabled them both to become more immersed in the themes underlying their superhero interests and to play them through in an extended way. Their sequences were often related to travel and transformation, which had previously been imperceptible to us because we stopped the play as soon as the noisy and combative superhero poses first appeared.

Jon and Magnus in fact utilized the transformatory powers at the heart of much superhero culture to empower them to make magical journeys to other places and to be brave and strong when they arrived. Their journeys were not bound by media scenarios but extended to incorporate their own agendas. Magnus was from Iceland and would often take Jon off on journeys to visit his homeland. Jon, in particular, was quite a withdrawn and physically cautious child in many respects and he found his voice and developed more confident movement skills by playing in this context. In Vygotskian terms 'In play it is as though he were a head taller than himself' (Vygotsky 1978: 102).

All three children quickly came to show greater confidence and their self-esteem was raised. They were legitimately able to explore other areas of the nursery in pursuit of their particular interests. They were able to develop fine motor and creative skills in their construction and prop making. They were more frequently found in the graphics or painting areas representing scenarios and objects from their play. Their oracy skills also developed because we were prepared to listen to whatever they wanted to tell us and, possibly related to this, they were more prepared to listen attentively to others.

Clearly involvement with these activities had a direct impact on all areas of development upon which cognitive growth is dependent. The resistant behaviour of these three boys more or less disappeared; we were no longer the enemy and they started to show a far greater sense of belonging. They were far more frequently seen to smile and laugh. They were no longer the socially excluded children of Pellegrini's (1988) study.

The border crossing noted in the play of some of the girls earlier in this chapter was also seen in Fred and Magnus's play. Approximately six months into our changed approach they both started to show an extensive interest in dressing up outside the war, weapon and super-hero play context. It was as if they had suddenly realized that they were allowed to try on absolutely any of the dressing-up clothes. This interest was noted by the practitioners and was initially fed by a new and copious supply of hats, which are a relatively safe item to experiment with.

Eventually the two boys started experimenting with the more unambiguously feminine clothes in our stock: skirts, handbags, frilly blouses and heels. Their border crossing in turn gave permission to many of the boys in the group to have a go and a great deal of fun was had by all. Such experimentation required courage: they knew that previously they would have laughed at another boy dressing up in this way. It was quite simply not something that boys did and would contradict the overgeneralization of gendered behaviour referred to in Chapter 2. Perhaps this was possible because they felt more accepted as boys and no longer had to define themselves in such a relational way against girls. Perhaps they simply felt more generally secure and confident and had an expectation of being valued and supported rather than judged. Whatever the reasons, a significant shift in their understandings of possible gender positionings had occurred.

Over time their interests broadened so that involvement in activities was not so consistently linked to weapon making or superhero play. It is possible that their enhanced self-esteem allowed them to countenance a higher level of risk taking so that doors into other areas of experience could be opened. This was seen to have a significantly beneficial effect on their well-being and overall development. Qualitative action research of this sort is not rocket science and, while a clear causal connection with our relaxation of zero tolerance cannot be claimed, as such developments could be ascribed simply to maturation, we can at least claim that relaxing zero tolerance did not hinder that process. Additionally, the accumulated practice wisdom of the team was that parallel progress in similar children simply through maturation was not their common experience.

Conclusion

When we reviewed our changed approach not one member of the team, even those who had been most sceptical at the beginning, felt that we should return to zero tolerance. Everyone felt that children had benefited and that their own professional practice and personal understanding had developed significantly. Parents/carers of those children with a persistent interest in war, weapon and superhero play were also relieved that their children were no longer viewed as problems and were delighted with improvements in both their learning and behaviour.

5

THE BIGGER PICTURE: A SUMMARY OF FINDINGS FROM 13 EARLY CHILDHOOD SETTINGS WHERE ZERO TOLERANCE HAS BEEN RELAXED

In Chapter 4 we looked at the experiences of practitioners in a single setting where zero tolerance of war, weapon and superhero play was dropped in response to a particular set of local dilemmas. These related to how this policy was impacting negatively on the play opportunities and well-being of a small group of young boys.

At the time when this change was being enacted members of the team did not consider that this piece of work might have significance for other early childhood settings: our agenda was specific to our context. It became clear, however, as our findings were disseminated, at first informally through discussion with other practitioners and subsequently through feedback to conference presentations and articles I was asked to write, that our dilemmas had common currency with early years practitioners around the country.

It is no exaggeration to say that I found myself inundated with requests to speak to groups of practitioners in a wide range of contexts: centre-based and local education authority in-service training days; workshops offered by professional associations; professional and academic conferences. Clearly we were not the only people troubled by the prescriptive nature of zero tolerance. On each occasion I was struck by the extent of common ground concerning both the patterns of children's interests and behaviours in relation to war, weapon and superhero play and the moral tensions experienced by the practitioners in settings operating zero tolerance.

As a result of attending these presentations and workshops a number of practitioners embarked on the process of reviewing and changing practice in their own settings. I have maintained contact with a number of these settings in order to monitor their experiences and to expand the data available to the early years community in relation to approaches to war, weapon and superhero play. I have also worked closely alongside four settings during the process of change. I came across two other settings where the practice of zero tolerance had already been relaxed for reasons similar to those expressed in Chapter 4. Data for this chapter has been drawn from questionnaires, interviews with individual practitioners and discussions with teams and from my own observations in some of those settings.

I will build on the previous chapter's description and analysis of the experiences of the setting relaxing zero tolerance by considering strands of evidence from 20 early years settings where similar changes have been made. The focus will be on the differences and similarities in both the approaches taken to practice and the impact of these strategies on children's play and well-being from practitioners' points of view.

When the outcome of the initial research first became public it was not only the early years community that took an interest. Newspapers, radio stations and television seized on the findings, in some cases simplifying and distorting them, suggesting that we were urging a return to gun play and had proved that it did children no harm. Some journalists wanted to film and photograph children and seemed insensitive to the vulnerability of young children and their families. It is as a result of those experiences and the wishes of settings concerned that I will be reporting findings from this wider group of settings with complete anonymity.

The sample

In this chapter we shall look at how the findings from questionnaires help us to gain an overview. We will develop themes as they emerge in greater depth from interview, discussion and observational data. It should be noted that I am continuing to collect information by all of these means and so the conclusions we shall explore here represent an overview to date and are not definitive. However, the patterns which are emerging across settings suggest that the evidence is robust and should significantly inform discussions within the early childhood community about policy and practice in relation to war, weapon and superhero play.

All the settings but one are local education authority-funded and represent a range of under-fives centres, nursery schools and nursery classes within primary schools. The majority are in inner London.

We shall look at responses from 18 completed questionnaires, which were received back from a total of 28 settings that had previously signalled their willingness to be contacted to follow up their progress. Thirteen settings reported that they had changed from a zero tolerance approach; two of them had done so before attending workshops or conferences. Four of these settings were in the early stages of change, returned incomplete questionnaires or are subject to more in-depth consideration later in this chapter.

Of the five settings reporting no change to practice only one states that it is still committed to zero tolerance as an appropriate policy. One setting had deferred change pending the completion of a new building; one team was already operating a more relaxed approach and didn't feel a need to make further changes; one team was working with 2 to 3-year-olds and did not find war, weapon and superhero play an issue; and the fifth setting was in the transitional stage of planning for change. What appears to be significant here is that only one setting out of the 18 that responded was sustaining a zero tolerance approach. This signals a level of concern and discomfort among practitioners with zero tolerance and a willingness to reflect on practice and consider alternative approaches. The issue is clearly live in the early childhood community.

Responses to the question asking practitioners to describe their current policy demonstrated an emphasis on allowing war, weapon and superhero play to take place within clear behaviour boundaries. Respondents were concerned with protecting children not involved in the play, one identifying the category of 'willing participants', and ensuring that no one was hurt. Two settings reported that the play was only allowed outside and one stated that no physical contact was allowed. Only one respondent chose to mention approaches to practice and 'extending [the play] through story telling and construction'. It may be that people associate the word policy with rules and guidelines and answered the question accordingly, or it may be a reflection of practitioners' anxiety about managing the play which led them to focus on these aspects.

This anxiety was a consistent feature of discussion among practitioners at workshops and also features in the literature concerning this area of play from outside England (Kuykendall 1995; Cupit 1996). The importance of boundaries is a recurrent theme across the sources of evidence and we shall examine this now in greater detail.

Boundaries

In Chapter 4 we looked at how the use of constructed weapons was allowed, provided that children did not shoot at people, and suggested that this boundary could be contested. It had been applied because it was as far as that team felt they could go at that particular time. This model has been taken on by some other settings and the feedback on the operation of this boundary is generally positive. It has proved to be a particularly supportive strategy in two settings where the heads of centre have reported that there is still some ambiguity concerning the change among staff and where focused support for the play comes from particular individual team members with developed skills in imaginative play. Operating the boundary in these contexts has reduced the volume of random and highly active gun play, has restored staff confidence and has allowed heads of centre to plan in-house development of the skills necessary to support and extend war, weapon and superhero play.

Other reported advantages of this boundary are that it appears to prompt the creation of imaginary foes, minimizes the intimidation of non-participant children and creates a discussion point about the line between fantasy and reality for adults and children. However, two settings where this boundary has been maintained are reviewing this for different but related reasons. In one setting there is concern about communicating the complexity of the boundary to the 2- and 3-year-olds and in another the same concern is felt in relation to children acquiring English as an additional language. The adults do not wish to put the children in a position of receiving reprimands for crossing a boundary which is logistically and linguistically difficult to communicate. In one of these settings the team is also feeling far more confident about managing and extending the play and they no longer feel that they need the boundary as a prop to their practice.

Another concern voiced in that setting is about the effects of this boundary on limiting children's access to the use of revival scenarios (the classic sequence of 'bang, bang, you're dead' in which the child falls over pretending to be dead and then comes back to life or is brought back to life). Some practitioners feel that this scenario is a dangerous one to encourage because it may foster the illusion that death is reversible and prevent children from distinguishing between the fantasy and reality of violent acts. An alternative reading is that such play allows children to explore schemas of transformation and functional dependency (cause and effect) (Athey 1990) rather than encouraging an artificial perspective on life and death, as perceived by some practitioners. As Pat Broadhead (1992: 49) observed in her work in this field:

> Perhaps we were wrong in attributing oppression, violence and death to gun play; after all, the young child does not understand the consequences of death in the way an adult does. We considered that gun play might be a powerful source of

emotional experience for children, playing out fears, experiencing thrills, anticipation and excitement in ways no other play can offer.

Some children will, of course, have experienced bereavement and will know, even if they do not understand, that the person who has died has not reappeared in their lives. Other children will have seen hospital dramas where people die and are resuscitated. Cultural contexts must be considered here. Some children may have been told that the dead are alive in heaven or that the dead are reincarnated. Some children in this way may in fact be utilizing knowledge from their culturally shaped reality in their fantasy play rather than acting from a false concept.

At another level it is also likely that some young children are prompted to explore revival scenarios as part of their development in relation to separation and attachment (Bowlby 1969). For many children, attending nursery is their first experience of being separated for extended periods of time from their parents/carers and they are learning that their attachment figure continues to exist when absent and will return safely at the end of the session. Revival sequences allow children to explore and play with this fundamental concern. For other children the exploration of cause and effect – if I do A then B will happen – may be more at the heart of this interest. Certainly for Darren, whose story featured in Chapter 3, revival scenarios were an important transitional area of play which served to extend his interests beyond gun play, and for many boys observed in this study it can be a link into hospital and rescue sequences. Such play clearly gives an opportunity to explore issues of care and nurture.

Setting a boundary on children pointing and using weapons directly against other people has clearly been a positive strategy in some settings, but one which has no absolute validity and may prove to be a transitional phase in some of them.

Empowerment

We shall turn now to a different approach taken in some settings, in which the model from the outset of relaxing zero tolerance has been one of empowerment. In these settings practitioners have opted to emphasize children's right to define the boundaries of their fantasy play provided that 'willing participants' respect the rights of those who do not wish to join in. In some settings this takes the form of children being told that they can only shoot at people involved in the game. In others the emphasis is on empowering children to say 'no' in a more general sense, when they do not like what is happening.

I have observed this strategy to be most effective in settings where a children's rights approach is embedded in both philosophy and practice and where practitioners are proactive in supporting children's ability to make decisions. As a practitioner in one such setting commented, 'It's about a vision, not just policy, because the ethos of the centre is not about suppressing children.' In this setting children are taught from their admission to the setting the maketon (a system of sign language) sign for 'no' and are encouraged to use it to support the verbal message and to ensure that their wishes are communicated to all children using the centre. This encourages children to be active agents in their play choices and practitioners report overall that they have minimal issues with behaviour management as children are supported in developing self-discipline.

They feel that this approach 'allows children to not go with the game sometimes and if this went on in primary and secondary we would have a very different society. We would have people who were empowered enough to say no when they're uncomfortable about something.' I have to reflect here on the accounts of those drawn in to committing acts of atrocity during the Second World War, who account for their actions by claiming that they were acting under orders. As early childhood practitioners we need to consider the value that is placed on children's compliance with our wishes and the repressive way we sometimes handle children's acts of resistance.

Another setting, in its first year of change, is building on this empowerment model by consulting with children about the kind of rules that they wish to be in place around war, weapon and superhero play. They are also engaged in a substantial staff development programme covering imaginative play, work with persona dolls and the Effective Early Learning project (Pascal *et al.* 1996), all of which they feel will enable them to support children's autonomous play, imaginative development and emotional well-being more effectively. They, in common with all the settings I have encountered in this research, see an open approach to war, weapon and superhero play in the broader context of children's rights and child-focused practice.

A further area of discussion within the field of boundaries has concerned the parallel rights and responsibilities of practitioners: should they play sword fights with children; shoot back in a gunfight game; feign death or injury when shot? Responses to these questions have again been diverse across settings. While some teams have felt that a consistent approach across the team is important, the majority have concluded that, provided all members of the team uphold a positive general response to war, weapon and superhero play, adults should be seen to be accorded the same choices that are being made available to children. Thus a team member saying 'No, I don't want to play this game, please don't shoot me' is simultaneously demonstrating diversity among adults and modelling resistance and choice to children.

Practitioners felt that children generally recognized the different interests and strengths of team members and often approached them for support differentially across the curriculum in any case. As one practitioner observed: 'It's fine with them and fine with us, because that's what life is like. Children know we're not all the same, we're not all clones of each other. It really is an important issue.'

A more open agenda of this sort also might mean that discussions about behaviour that a child or adult might find unacceptable will be less formulaic and more focused on the diversity of human feelings and responses. Clearly this approach has to be supported by the consistent and fair application of a behaviour policy known and understood by both children and adults, which emphasizes respect for others and the development of self-discipline in individual children.

Who plays? A distorted perception?

We shall return now to the questionnaire responses. Practitioners were asked to quantify the number of children in their class group who had a persistent interest in war, weapon and superhero play. The figures ranged from four to eight in an average group size of 26. All respondents specified that these were boys. This is consistent with practitioner responses at workshops and in interviews, in which they will refer to a handful or a few boys in each year's intake who show a significant interest. While these estimates match my own practice experience I was surprised to discover that when I compared incidents of war, weapon and superhero play from video recordings in two settings with those children named as the key protagonists by the centre teams I identified many more children who were involved in this area of play than those named.

This led to extensive reflection and discussion among the two teams and perhaps takes us back to the point made in Chapter 2 concerning distortions in practitioners' perceptions of play fighting and of the boys involved in this area of play. I noted, when asking practitioners to name these children in the two settings, that certain names tripped off the tongue, often with comments indicating that the child might otherwise present challenging behaviour. When comparing these lists of names with the video data the named children all appeared. However, also engaged in war, weapon and superhero play alongside them or in different play groups were between two and three times as many children whose play was less likely to attract attention (perhaps it was quieter or out of clear view) and who were generally seen to be settled, helpful and cooperative.

And the girls?

A similar discrepancy came to light in relation to a question concerning whether relaxing zero tolerance had impacted on the involvement of girls in this area of play. Only two settings reported that there had been an increase in the involvement of girls, although the picture did become a little more substantial in the interview material. However, observations made in the same two settings as referred to above revealed that a number of girls were in fact involved in different aspects of war, weapon and superhero play. A brief description of one such episode may help to illustrate why such examples of girls' participation in war, weapon and superhero play may often go unnoticed.

A group of five girls, Chantal, Tahiba, Katie, Amina and Sara, were playing in the outside playhouse. A solitary boy, Ahmed, approached the window of the house and gave an almighty roar. A classic monster chase sequence immediately sprang to life. The girls plotted their strategy and agreed to chase the monster away. They did not, however, all leave the playhouse unarmed. Tahiba and Katie seized two toy drills and wielded them gun fashion. Chantal and Amina clipped together lengths of construction materials from a box just outside the house and off they all ran in hot pursuit of the monster. They ran in a circuit several times around the outdoor area and I watched carefully to see what use would be made of the weapons. I also observed the practitioners in the playground to see if any noticed that there was an armed gang of girls chasing around the playground, as, given previous feedback, this would be a rare occurrence. Admittedly the guns were constructed in a straight line and did not have the usual L shape, and the drills could have been mistaken for drills even though they were obviously not being used as such.

The girls finally surrounded the monster and the weapons were discharged with appropriate sound effects. When I casually asked Chantal what she had in her hand she told me that it was a magic stick that turned monsters into parrots. Was this said simply to pacify me, given that zero tolerance had only recently been dropped, or was it a dual-purpose object representing a gun as a kind of magic wand? More to the point, did the practitioners fail to identify such incidences of war, weapon and superhero play because they assumed that the constructions were indeed magic wands or do assumptions bias our perceptions? This particular observation did make me wonder why magic wands, which can inflict terrible fantasy pain, contortions and death, are considered acceptable when fantasy guns and swords are not.

Interestingly, my work has generated numerous examples of boys creating guns with the same transformatory powers as magic wands. This all suggests that a common theme of magic powers and of experiencing power in a fantasy realm can be traced across gendered play forms. After all, in traditional girls' fantasy games is there not usually a good witch or fairy locked in battle with an evil counterpart much as we find in superhero and fiend scenarios? There will be further discussion of girls' involvement in war, weapon and superhero play in Chapter 6.

More war, weapon and superhero play?

Questionnaire respondents were also asked to comment on whether they thought there was more war, weapon and superhero play after zero tolerance had been relaxed. Two settings felt that there had been more, one less, perceptions of the team differed in the fourth setting and the remaining five reported that levels were the same. Settings had not been asked to attempt before and after incidence counting and so the responses are impressionistic. However, the impression from two-thirds of the settings is that there was no major or sustained escalation in the volume of war, weapon and superhero play. The one setting in which I observed a substantial and sustained escalation of war, weapon and superhero play had for some months before my involvement been maintaining a blind eye policy, so that the play had not been supported or extended. One particular child, Darren, discussed in Chapter 3, had an almost exclusive interest in war, weapon and superhero play and had doubtless influenced dynamics in the group in the early stages of transition.

The team in this setting was split in terms of support for the policy change and the majority of team members were not proactive in planning for or supporting children's observed play interests, especially in relation to imaginative play. There had also been a lack of clarity concerning the application of the behaviour policy in relation to the play. After behaviour boundaries had been re-established and some of the team started working more proactively the volume of war, weapon and superhero play started to diminish. Darren also joined the reception class at the same time, but there were several other children with a 'daily' interest in this play and the team did not feel that the reduction in volume related purely to his departure.

Some settings reported that there had been an initial escalation of war, weapon and superhero play, much as had been experienced in the setting discussed in Chapter 4. One of the settings reporting that the volume had increased noted that this was probably because the play was now less secretive and therefore more observable.

More aggression?

Respondents were also asked to comment on whether they felt that relaxing zero tolerance had impacted on levels of real aggressive incidents. This question is of key importance both because of the level of anxiety consistently shown by practitioners about managing behaviour after relaxing zero tolerance and also because of the implicit assumption held by many people that aggressive play scenarios are causally related to aggressive behaviour. Only one setting indicated that there had been some real fights between boys, but at a subsequent interview the acting head of centre stated that there had not been an overall increase in the amount of real aggression over time. The other eight responses, all affirming that there had been no increase in incidents of real aggression, are tabulated below.

Do you think that changing policy has had any effect on levels of real aggression or violent play?
There's not much difference.
There's very little anyway as we are a private school with space and good adult to child ratios.
There's been no increase.
Real aggression has lessened and violent play is seen in a different light – the ground rules are enforced.
There's no effect. The sword and superhero play isn't really aggressive.
There's very little aggressive play.
The play is more positive because of adult awareness.
No.

Eight out of nine settings felt that relaxing zero tolerance had been positive

Another question asked whether practitioners felt that the changes had been positive overall. Eight out of nine responded unequivocally yes and the ninth said that they were unsure. A significant majority were thus overridingly positive about relaxing zero tolerance despite the challenges that such a change had brought. Respondents were invited to comment further and six chose to do so.

We shall look at these comments (numbered 1–6) below. They are expanded by reference to findings from interviews and team discussions, with links being made to theoretical points made in earlier chapters. There are also responses drawn from an additional question asking if practitioners felt there had been a perceptible change in the well-being and development of individual boys with a persistent interest as there is a crossover in some of the material.

The most striking feature of these comments overall is that all but one setting chose to comment on developments within imaginative play. The forms of the play itself will be further explored in Chapter 6. This clearly lends support to the arguments we explored in Chapter 3 concerning the potential in relaxing zero tolerance for fostering the imaginative growth of those boys with a persistent interest in war, weapon and superhero play.

1 Some children are very creative but there always seems to be a group who get over-excited and do not develop their play even with an adult joining in.

The element of reservation expressed in this comment had resonance with the experience of some practitioners interviewed. In some situations this difficulty dissipated over time as the adults became more resourceful or as the children concerned moved on to other play interests or were more able to respond to extension as the novelty of their new freedom wore off. Commonly these practitioners felt at a loss in terms of extending the play, as they were not familiar or comfortable with the play forms.

Many teams have been proactive in their own development and have extended their range of strategies:

- One centre head invested in an extensive set of toy soldiers and action figures in an attempt to resolve this difficulty and found that two boys who had been consistently involved in repetitive and physically active war play scenarios spent an hour and a half engaged in small world narrative play with these figures.

- Other settings have found that enhanced stocks of dressing-up clothes, particularly capes, made accessible outside the home corner, have made a significant difference.
- In other contexts it has been found helpful to focus more extensively on the child/children involved and to consider what other social agenda might be influencing the child/children's play.
- In settings where practitioners have knowledge of schema theory, patterns of repeated behaviour which can be utilized to support learning (Athey 1990), they have found it helpful to analyse the play accordingly and support the underlying schema, frequently a trajectory schema, an interest in the movement of a real or imaginary object through space, for example throwing.

What is common to the responses made by teams to this difficulty is that the play form (war, weapon and superhero play) is separated from the behaviour and banning the play is no longer seen as supportive to the child. War, weapon and superhero play is no longer seen as being inevitably associated with aggressive behaviour.

2 There is more free-flow play among boys and friendships have been made through Batman and Robin combinations.

This enhancement of social skills was noted with Fred, Hakim and Jon in Chapter 4 and also in the cameo of Darren in Chapter 3. It was also the subject of frequent comment in interviews. Examples from experience in two settings are quoted below:

> I think there were people who were included more – boys who were into that [war, weapon and superhero play] and using it as a vehicle for stories . . . it gave them a leadership role, 'I know how to make one of those, I'll show you.' That was giving status to someone who was operating on the outside.

> I think one of the most useful things about superhero play is that it can be very, very simple – just chasing. And that means that children who feel totally insecure can be part of that – children when they are admitted, that can be the first game. That seems to be quite crucial. They're watching it on the tele and they see other people playing and all they've got to do is put a cloak on.

I witnessed many such interchanges during my observation visits to settings. I feel that this is perhaps one of the most significant findings of the research to date, because it relates so closely to the children identified as being at risk of developing aggressive behaviour because of their lack of both social status and imaginative development (Pellegrini 1988; Singer 1994; Dunn and Hughes 2001).

One such child, diagnosed as having Attention Deficit and Hyperactivity Disorder (ADHD), had been previously excluded from three early years settings. ADHD is a controversial diagnosis that is increasingly being made of younger and younger children displaying unsettled and challenging behaviour. The diagnosis frequently leads to the prescription of Ritalin to control the behaviour. This drug is also the source of much controversy as there are concerns about its long-term use and possible side effects. This child's parents were extremely relieved by the impact of policy change on their son's behaviour and social status.

Other settings similarly reported improvements in the behaviour of children having behaviour-related special needs and those on the autistic spectrum.

The following observation relating to an extended superhero play project illustrates the point:

> One of the children, who took the lead a lot of the time, is a child diagnosed as ADHD and he would have terrific tantrums, but he didn't during the duration of the play.

The potential of war, weapon and superhero play for enhancing social skills was also noted by Pat Broadhead (1992: 48) in her research in this area:

> I then observed some extended highly social play bouts involving gun play . . . I noted . . . that making and pointing a gun at another child facilitated eye contact and smiles, occasionally leading to a 'coming together' of unfamiliar peers.

A number of settings also identified particular benefits to boys acquiring English as an additional language. Two examples appear below:

> [War, weapon and superhero play] allowed a new boy with very little English to join in play with peers.

> Two boys new to English had a real interest and our new approach meant we could accept their play.

The former situation is probably a reflection of the accessibility of the play form discussed above, but in the latter the relaxation of zero tolerance meant that children who might already feel culturally and linguistically alienated did not have to encounter further alienation as a result of their play interests.

3 This is a big part of boys' imaginary lives.

This comment signals a renewed interest in, and respect towards, the play interests of some young boys. It reflects back to a comment quoted earlier in this chapter, which observed that 'The play is more positive, because of adult awareness.'

4 There is more well-supported superhero play with well-made props and all role-play situations have improved with the increased use of technology.

Some comments recorded in response to the question about individual benefits, and others in interviews, made similar points (see Appendix, question 9):

> This often introduces children into new areas in the nursery through extension.

> Many boys turned their attention to technology and were inventive making swords and guns and other trajectory stuff.

> They'd go into the workshop – they didn't really venture there before then – to make props to go with their play. The props were mainly swords but they were extending their ideas. They weren't just picking up a plank of wood, they were choosing materials.

> There was a particular group of boys – to get them to come in and sit down at a table would be impossible, but if you were going to do a Superman or Batman story or pictures they were there and they would be there for the whole session. Or building a Batman boat – you could get them into every area through that.

These comments all suggest that, as we found with Fred, Hakim and Jon in Chapter 4, a more relaxed approach to war, weapon and superhero play can enhance the all-round development of children with a particular interest in this area of play by providing an access route to all areas of the Foundation Stage (QCA 2000) curriculum. This approach is consistent with good early childhood practice: the notion that we should find the spark that ignites a child's interest and keep it burning. To light such a fire at this stage of a child's educational experience is surely a major raison d'être of all early childhood practitioners and is particularly pertinent in relation to that group of young boys who may otherwise grow up to be disaffected and failing adolescents. The learning potential of war, weapon and superhero play is also noted by Cupit (1996: 24), writing from the Australian context:

> If, as many assert . . . children learn through play, we must identify the learning potential of any example of superhero play and respond as we would to any other play event. This may mean discussion of issues raised by the play, deliberate intrusion of new and challenging play components, or providing extension activities. It will mean entering actively into the play, understanding its themes, researching its language and concepts and treating it not as a disruption to be prevented, but as another gateway for learning.

The final sentence of this quote has resonance with a common difficulty experienced in many settings which has been previously referred to, of the challenge of 'entering actively into the play' (Cupit 1996: 24) and supporting it. The most effective means to date of resolving this difficulty has been through the exchange of experiences between settings through a war, weapon and superhero play forum, which has recently been set up, and through team in-service training on imaginative play. Some strategies have been shared in this chapter and others will be considered in the following chapter.

5 Some boys have more fun now at nursery and their play is more imaginative with more boys dressing up; some play princes.

A practitioner from another setting echoed this with an observation strikingly similar to Fred's exploration of dressing up in Chapter 4:

> . . . at the end we were getting two boys putting on long leather boots, high heel shoes – never seen that before – dressing up in skirts, ethnic clothes and filling bags with things from the home corner and taking them outside on to the truck and going off on their holiday.

It is encouraging to find, among the general feedback concerning the enhancement of imaginative play, one other clear example of gender role border crossing facilitated by the relaxation of zero tolerance.

6 There is less tension, fewer times adults have to say 'no'. Children are not hiding to make guns and can be honest.

The first example of the benefit described above relates to the atmosphere within a setting, which clearly impacts positively on both adults and children. This benefit was noted in the setting discussed in Chapter 4 where one practitioner observed that she felt 'more relaxed, because I am not constantly telling children off', and was similarly noted in a third setting:

> It's freed everything up, it's freed people up, it's freed people's time up – everything is flowing more easily.

Conclusion

The second element of comment 6 concerning the facilitation of honesty leads me to the conclusion of this chapter. Following the events of 11 September 2001 I was thrown into a state of high anxiety about the nature of my research work and had to revisit many of the moral issues that had kept me in close allegiance to a zero tolerance approach to war, weapon and superhero play for so many years.

During this period of reflection I was visiting a number of settings and was noting how they were supporting children in responding to these events. I saw little evidence of a proactive response except in the two settings which had been relaxing zero tolerance for the longest time spans, five and three years respectively. The following comments made in those settings reaffirmed my commitment to challenging a policy which inherently inhibits children's opportunities to openly re-enact, process and discuss real events, not just the fantasy world of cartoons and media merchandising, which impinge on their developing construction of the world. Practitioners in both settings emphasized the fact that relaxing zero tolerance was not a finite event, but was an ongoing process of responding to children's needs and interests in an open, dynamic and non-judgemental way: 'A vision, not just a policy' (practitioner quoted earlier in this chapter).

> You need to keep revisiting things, especially when there are issues like the current issue of terrorism. But the important thing is that we are enabling children to talk about what is happening, so that they can make sense of where they are getting the images from.

I think since September 11th it's [war, weapon and superhero play] really escalated big time. If we were not allowing guns what would we be doing now? Not allowing them to express what they're feeling and seeing. And we put pictures up to give them a channel to talk about it. It happened and it's amazing how much our children took it in and were talking about it and re-enacting it.

I hope that the voices of the practitioners heard in this chapter have demonstrated that the positive experiences of the setting outlined in Chapter 4 are not unique and are at least sufficient to promote wide and reflective discussion within the early childhood community about diverse and innovative approaches to war, weapon and superhero play.

6

WAR, WEAPON AND SUPERHERO PLAY: WHAT DOES IT LOOK LIKE?

Let us return to the sequence with Fred and Hakim that opened Chapter 1, imagining that the setting has relaxed its zero tolerance approach to war, weapon and superhero play and that practitioners are open to this play and 'observe, support and extend' it (Bruce 1997b: 97).

It is close to the beginning of a session in a nursery classroom. Most of the children have arrived and they are settling down to their chosen activities. Out of the corner of her eye an early years practitioner notices two boys on the other side of the room playing quietly in the construction area. There are no other adults close by. Fred is toting an elaborate weapon carefully assembled from Mobilo (rigid plastic components in a variety of 2D and 3D square and rectangular configurations that are joined by fixed or articulated connectors). It has a folding handle and flip-up sight with two barrel-shaped projections, one positioned above the other. He takes aim through his sight at Hakim who is crouching behind an enclosure of hollow blocks they have just built together. Hakim is holding a small curved unit block; there is no mistaking from his pose and the way he holds it that in his mind it represents a gun.

They are smiling. Simultaneously they cry out 'peow, peow, peow' and start to chase each other in a circle around the enclosure. After a while Hakim announces to his friend that he would like a different gun but can't make one. Fred says, 'I can show you' and they head over to the box of Mobilo. They spend 10 minutes making the new gun. At first Fred, the expert, models and makes a basic framework and then his friend joins in, adding the elaborations he desires, which includes a 'picture thing', probably a digital image screen, attached to the side.

All the while they are chatting and a wealth of comparative, but not competitive, language can be heard – bigger, longer, wider. Gina has by this time crossed the room and gently asks about their constructions. The boys proudly point out the features of their constructions. Gina is particularly impressed when they tell her that the top barrel puts people to sleep and that the bottom barrel fires a magic potion into baddies' brains and makes them good. Gina praises their ingenuity and comments that it's great to see them making guns that don't kill. They smile broadly and ask if they can keep their constructions to show their parents at home time. She responds positively and also suggests that when they have finished their game they could find her to have a photo of their weapons taken and tell her a story about them. They nod enthusiastically, return to their play, but they do indeed go and seek her out later in the session and tell her a story about their adventures, which she writes down.

Unknown territory

For many early childhood practitioners extended war, weapon and superhero play is unknown territory, because the operation of zero tolerance has meant that we only have glimpses of the beginnings of the play before we intercept it. Over the past four years I have had the privilege of observing a substantial amount of extended sequences of play myself in a variety of settings, as well as being party to practitioners' observations.

In Chapter 5 practitioners describing the benefits of a relaxed approached to war, weapon and superhero play consistently emphasized the development of imaginative play, alongside social development, as a major gain. In Chapter 3 the importance of the development of imaginative play in relation to war, weapon and superhero play was considered in some depth. In this chapter my aim is to categorize some of the common features, themes and forms of war, weapon and superhero play that emerge when the play is allowed to develop, with a particular focus on the ways in which the play can be identified as imaginative.

In order to keep in mind the possible relevance of war, weapon and superhero play as a springboard to imaginative development, a central premise of this book, we shall return to the work of Judy Dunn and Claire Hughes (2001) referred to in Chapter 3. Their findings show that children who utilize violent play themes are less frequently involved in pretend play than children who utilize other themes and that children who utilise violent play themes at age 4 are more likely to demonstrate anti-social behaviour at age 6. They do not claim that there is a causative relationship between these factors and, as I have done throughout this book, they emphasize the importance of identifying which other features of children's lives give rise to their interest in violent play themes in the first instance.

The identification of causative factors must continue to exercise researchers in the field, but in the interim I believe we have a professional responsibility to work at the interface of these associative connections in an effort to minimize the negative outcomes at age 6 that have been reported by Dunn and Hughes (2001).

It is important to note that Dunn and Hughes do not identify the approach taken to violent play themes in the settings they researched, or state whether attempts were made to support and extend the play. My argument is that war, weapon and superhero play can be used as a platform to extend and develop the imaginative play capabilities of some of those hard-to-manage children identified as being at risk in Dunn and Hughes's work in order to avoid the negative social outcomes noted in those children at the age of 6.

We must also bear in mind that far from all of the children who demonstrate a persistent interest in war, weapon and superhero play are at risk from other social factors of developing aggressive or anti-social behaviour. My observations indicate that such children are a minority and that most children who choose such play themes, when a choice is available to them, show no inclination towards direct aggression within or beyond their play scenarios.

Supporting imaginative play   ■

We need to make a link here with the work of those who demonstrate that appropriate adult support and intervention can impact on children's ability to engage with pretend play. Smilansky and Shefatya (1990) are particularly concerned with the relationship between socio-economic background, frequency of socio-dramatic play and academic outcomes. While there are other overlaps with the themes of this book which could be explored, my particular concern here is with their evidence of benefit to those children showing low levels of participation in socio-dramatic play from sensitive adult intervention. Smilansky and Shefatya (1990: xii) note that:

> . . . a large body of research has accumulated, conducted by ourselves and others in the United States, the United Kingdom and in Israel. These studies provide cross-cultural support for our contentions about the existence of differences in sociodramatic play behaviour with regard to socio-economic background; they

also support our suggestions about the relevance of such play for school-related behaviour and achievement and about the *feasibility of 'teaching' social make-believe play by means of short term adult intervention using a variety of methods* (my emphasis). Moreover, it has been demonstrated that there is transfer from such intervention to a variety of cognitive, creative, socio-emotional and academic skills.

The key link I am making in this way between my work and that of Dunn and Hughes (2001) is that children's play behaviour is not carved in stone and is amenable to sensitive practitioners, like sculptors, working with, rather than against the grain of children's play. This notion is further supported with reference to play more generally by Bruce (1997b: 97):

> The essence of adults and children developing play together is for the adult to 'observe, support and extend the play' (Bruce 1997). Observation means using theory and research to inform both on-the-spot and reflective understanding about play between adults and children. Supporting begins where the child is and with what the child can do. Extending might be to give help with physical materials, create space, give time, dialogue and converse about the play idea, or help with access strategies for the child to enter into the play with other children. Extending also involves sensitivity and adding appropriately stimulating material provision, and the encouragement of the child's autonomous learning. Both children and adults must value and learn to understand what is needed in play. Otherwise play won't work.

We will now take a closer look at what war, weapon and superhero play looks like in the classroom and in the playground, the imaginative elements of that play, and the kind of adult support and intervention that can help to extend and give added value to that play. It is not possible within the boundaries of my research to quantify a precise relationship between the amount and nature of support given and the benefits noted to particular children, particularly given that some gains were noted in settings where practitioners felt, or I observed, that limited support to the play had been given. However, the examination that follows of the play that developed and examples of support given should help to illuminate positive features of practice in this area.

In order to make the material manageable we will be looking at common features of the play that emerges in roughly drawn

categories. These categories are not discrete and there are many overlaps and continuities from one into another. I will highlight some of
the connections as the categories unfold.

Construction

In the weeks immediately after relaxing zero tolerance one of the first
areas of play in which practitioners have noted significant development in terms of both volume and range is that of construction, using
both construction kits and modelling in the technology area. Given
that one of the most common points of interception in war, weapon
and superhero play for practitioners operating zero tolerance is the
construction of a weapon, we should not be surprised that this is one
of the first areas in which children's activity escalates once the ban is
lifted. What is perhaps more surprising is the rapid sophistication of
the designs of weapons constructed.

Practitioners defending zero tolerance will often cite examples of
children clipping together two pieces of lego into a gun shape as indicating the low level of imaginative functioning involved. Observations across time and across settings clearly indicate that such
'low-level' construction is the product of children operating under the
constraints of disapproval and time limitations.

A common reflection across settings concerned the extent to which
the properties of the available materials affected the nature of the
constructions made. In a nutshell this means both that some construction kits lend themselves more readily to weapon making and
that the properties of some kits allow for greater diversity in construction. For example, the articulation possibilities of Mobilo can be used
to add features that flip up and possibly thus extend the functions of
the weapon made. As one child was heard to say, excitedly seeking
attention for his latest construction, 'Look, a phone and gun, a phone
and gun.'

Other kits more readily offer the possibility of extending length and
children have been observed using these materials to construct 'long
swords' and 'long guns', experimenting to see how long they can
make their constructions before they collapse at the first attempt to
wave them in the air. I have observed many sequences of play in which
children constantly refine and redesign their constructed weapons in
order to resolve the difficulties they experience when using them.

Connexion offers a completely different range of design possibilities
in terms of length and the opportunity to intersect vertical, horizontal
and diagonal connections. As with Mobilo, this enables children to
create constructions which have a wide variety of functions.

Some practitioners have expressed anxiety about the effect of contagion on children's play after zero tolerance has been relaxed, so that children who had previously shown no interest in war, weapon and superhero play would be drawn in to this area of play. While some degree of imitation is observable, the diversity of children's weapon construction strongly suggests that children are working to their own play agendas and that they had previously been compliant rather than disinterested.

My observations also suggest that the proliferation of war, weapon and superhero play was greater in settings where practitioners took more of a laissez-faire than involved stance after zero tolerance had been relaxed. Where practitioners supported and extended the play (Bruce 1997b) they seemed more likely to identify an underlying theme or interest like pirates or other adventure scenarios in which weapons played a secondary role. Where children's diverse needs and interests form the basis of the curriculum there is far less opportunity for purely imitative play to persist. Clearly, imitative play has an important part to play in children's learning and entry into group situations, but there needs to be a balance with autonomy and innovation.

The development in the diverse range of children's three dimensional weapon construction offered evidence of children's creative, imaginative and manipulative skills. Once children had realized that they were not going to be interrupted in their endeavours, or chastised for them, they quickly moved beyond the simple two brick, handle and barrel construction. Many of the boys, who had not been seen to concentrate for extended periods on any tasks, were frequently observed to spend between four and fifteen minutes constructing a weapon from construction kit materials. This indicates a high level of involvement, which is seen by many to indicate that children are learning at a deep level (Pascal *et al.* 1996; Laevers *et al.* 1997).

This activity was often highly collaborative and involved dialogue between children, as described in the opening sequence of this chapter, as well as prompting the use of a range of comparative mathematical language, the exploration of symmetry, the exploration of the properties of the materials being used and development of the fine motor skills required to manipulate those materials. Over weeks children were seen to construct with increasing confidence and sophistication. During the course of a session children would be observed to revisit the construction area, add to their construction, dismantle it and remodel it with refinements or produce a completely new model, the level of challenge rising consistently.

From the concrete to the abstract

At this point we need to return to the assertion made consistently in this book about the extremely significant difference between children playing with manufactured toy weapons and constructing their own. A manufactured toy weapon dictates to the child how he or she should play with it. Its functions are defined by the manufacturer and not the child: a toy gun is to be pointed and shot; a sword to be waved and thrust. A manufactured weapon colonizes or directs a child's imaginative engagement, whereas I believe the act of construction activates a child's imagination in a very different way. My research is concerned with children constructing their own weapons and I do not advocate that early years settings should provide manufactured toy weapons or that children should be allowed to bring these in from home.

Children engaged in construction in the ways described above are, in Vygotskian (1978) terms, moving towards abstract thinking, a crucial element of imaginative functioning. Drawing on the work of Lewin, Vygotsky describes how very young children are initially bound by the concrete world (1978: 96):

> . . . things dictate to the child what he must do: a door demands to be opened and closed, a staircase to be climbed, a bell to be rung. In short, things have . . . an inherent motivating force with respect to a very young child's actions and . . . extensively determine the child's behaviour . . .

Vygotsky views representational play as a crucial development in childhood, which enables children to move beyond the limitations of their immediate situation and object-focused language towards the manipulation of language and ideas in abstract thought:

> But in play, things lose their determining force. The child sees one thing but acts differently in relation to what he sees. Thus a condition is reached in which the child begins to act independently of what he sees . . . In play thought is separated from objects and action arises from ideas rather than from things: a piece of wood begins to be a doll and a stick becomes a horse.
>
> (Vygotsky 1978: 96–7)

According to this analysis, the child playing with a manufactured toy gun is motivated by the object, whereas the child involved in constructing a weapon is acting on an idea using materials which can undergo a series of transformations determined by the child's imagination.

This leads us back to considering the imaginative element of the children's constructions described earlier in this section. A visual analysis of the diversity of those constructions only gives us a limited view of imaginative function, the tip of the iceberg. To begin to appreciate more fully the extent to which imaginative thought preceded action for these children we must delve into the realms of language. The key lies in the verbal descriptions given by children to practitioners of the features and functions of their models.

Talking to children

This simultaneously takes us back to the territory of support and extension. We are only going to know what children think and intend if we invite and enter dialogue with them. This dialogue in turn produces the wherewithal for increasing challenge to individual children, planned resourcing and extension activities and the consequent broadening of children's interests and skills. First we will look at some examples of what children told us about their constructions and we will then look at examples of responsive practice.

Table 6.1 Children talking about their constructed weapons

1	I've got a gun that shoots bad men.
2	It kills baddies.
3	This isn't a gun, it's a toy – real guns kill.
4	If you press this button it goes peow and kills people and if you press this button it goes brrr and makes everybody alive.
5	It's a reviver, it shoots people then it brings people alive.
6	This sword chops down trees.
7	This gun can cut metal and trees.
8	Mine's a laser . . . it can zap you to another country.
9	It's a magic stick . . . it turns monsters into parrots . . . no, a duck.
10	My gun's a camera too.
11	I shoot stones.
12	It's a bubble shaker, it kills the baddies. The good chocolate comes out here and the bad chocolate for the baddies comes out here and you hold it here and go brrrrr.

These comments were elicited in the context of construction or the play which immediately followed, using the weapon as a prop. Some comments were made in brief, two- to three-turn exchanges with adults; others formed part of a more extended dialogue. Regardless of whether such opportunities were exploited on the occasion of the observation, each comment represents an opportunity for extended dialogue and we will look shortly at an example of one such exchange.

One feature of these exchanges that I noted in settings where zero tolerance had been recently relaxed was the body language between child and adult. Initially, when the adult signalled an interest in the child's construction, the child would appear wary and maintain physical distance. As the adult persisted and the child became convinced that the adult interest was authentic and positive the child would smile and move towards the adult and begin to describe his or her construction in a more animated way, using more sophisticated language. Clearly there is a window of opportunity here both to expand our understanding of children's thinking in this area of play and to extend that thinking through dialogue, but only if we choose to open that window.

The comments, chosen as a representative example across settings, all point to diverse imaginary worlds inside the children's minds, beyond the real aggressive intent, which the constructed object might at first sight represent to the practitioner.

Comments 1, 2 and 4, which refer directly to killing, are directed at imaginary and amorphous baddies. In the many conversations I have had with children in an attempt to find out more about the baddies, children will overwhelmingly characterize them as ghosts, monsters or wild animals. Despite the concerns frequently expressed by practitioners and parents about the escalating influence of violent media scenarios on young children I have rarely heard children cite characters from TV or video series as the baddie. Children's characterization of the baddies in their fantasies certainly warrants further investigation, but it appears that young children are still predominantly haunted by the same archetypal bogeymen as previous generations.

I would like to share here an anecdote from the personal experience of a journalist colleague, which reinforced for me the need that many children have to feel powerful against the fantasy foes of their nightmares. Her 3-year-old son, not an aggressive child, developed an interest in gun play when he started at playgroup. This interest brought down the disapproval of the playgroup organizer on both her own and her son's head, and generated a loss of self-esteem for the child and made it hard for him to develop a positive gender identity: he felt like a bad boy.

In the midst of this difficult time he started to have nightmares about being chased by dinosaurs, which escalated to the level of night terrors. My colleague sought advice from friends and attempted to help her son think of happier scenarios as he fell asleep to try to chase the nightmares away. Eventually he lost patience with his mum's well-intentioned efforts and declared that he needed guns in his dreams to stop the dinosaurs getting him. The tensions about weapon play that had coalesced around him had prevented him from arming himself as a powerless child against terrifying attacks in his dreams.

Just pretending

Comment 3, 'This isn't a gun, it's a toy – real guns kill', was echoed again and again by children across settings:

> We're just pretending.
> It's a pretend gun.
> It doesn't really hurt.

Clearly, we can learn much from listening to children's assertions that their constructed weapons may exist as real objects in the material world, but have powers that reside only in the world of dreams and fantasies.

Comments 4 and 5 reflect the theme referred to in Chapter 3 of revival, which I found being played out in all settings. As suggested there, this theme has a number of possible roots:

- the exploration of attachment and separation;
- exploration of concepts of life and death;
- cultural and religious influences concerning afterlife and reincarnation;
- transformation;
- influence of hospital dramas, where resuscitation is a frequent theme.

Given that as adults such mysteries of life, death and evil continue to exercise us throughout life, we should not minimize the human weight of such issues when they emerge in children's play. Perhaps in order to explore fragility safely children need to sense the possibility of resilience.

Similar transformatory powers are also attributed to the weapons described in comments 8, 9 and 12. Such statements also indicate a conflation of the technological and magical in children's imaginary lives. For young children it is rational to run these things together. If it is possible to illuminate darkness at the flick of a switch, why should it not be possible to imagine zapping someone to a different country with a laser? We could imagine that for our not so distant ancestors the possibility of air travel would reside in the same realm of fantasy. The mobile 'phone that my teenage daughter takes for granted was the stuff of science fiction in my youth.

Associating magical powers with scientific and technological fantasies and realities may be an act of meaning making appropriate to the level of knowledge and understanding of most 3- to 4-year-old children who are in the early stages of exploring cause and effect and how things work. Magic is the perfect transitional explanation for whatever children might find currently incomprehensible, a buffer to make the chaos and confusion of reality manageable, a security and sanity blanket. It may also help children to make sense of living in a world where everything still appears to be possible and to grow into adults with real transformatory powers: to turn the story in their heads into a book; to turn cloth into clothes; seeds into plants; electronic impulses into global communication; lasers into healing sources and, perhaps, swords into ploughshares.

> Much of children's exploration of the magical or miraculous necessarily takes place in their imagination, nurtured by the surrounding culture. In the context of fiction and also religion, they are led to think about various transformations and capacities that would ordinarily be impossible. Occasionally, however . . . their imaginative exploration is translated into a half-belief that everyday reality might also violate its customary causal regularities. Children mostly live in the ordinary world and expect mundane causal principles to hold sway, but, like adults, that does not prevent them from speculating and even hoping that it might be otherwise.
>
> (Harris 2000: 183)

I think it is important to return again to the work of Dunn and Hughes (2001) at this point. They noted that a significant difference between the hard-to-manage children and the control group that they observed was that the level of use of magical themes within the children's pretend play was higher in the control group. Their categorization of magical themes seemed to relate chiefly to fairytale themes or the more traditional territory of magic spells. However, I noted on more than one occasion when interacting with hard-to-manage children in fantasy sequences that they were consistently open to suggestions that powerful magic tokens, pieces of bark chippings for example, could help to fend off foes. Within these sequences weapons are rarely discharged and their role diminishes. It would be useful to research systematically over a period of time the extent to which children take on the substitution of magic power for the imaginary firepower of their weapons and to see if such changes correlated with improved social outcomes at a later stage.

Comments 6, 7, 10 and 11 focus more on functional aspects of the constructed weapons, with a stronger relationship to the child's primary or secondary experience. The unifying link is that no intent to harm or kill others is expressed: the weapons are seen as being useful tools – this sword chops down trees; this gun can cut metal and trees. Again, adults' assumptions about intent to harm are challenged by the children's own words.

Moving on to consider responsive practice towards comments 1–11, the common shift was in the opening of dialogue between practitioners and children. These comments were all noted in settings which had recently introduced a change of policy. While they did not, in all cases, directly lead to extension work on those occasions, they were significant events in terms of laying the ground for the practitioners concerned to realize that children's weapon constructions were not mindless acts. It was also significant for the children concerned to realize that their creative efforts were being noted and that their constructions were no longer taboo.

It is important that we do not undervalue the impact of these exchanges, in which practitioners had moved beyond prescriptive and disparaging responses as well as the token 'Yes, that's very nice' response. They had spent time and effort encouraging children to share their thoughts. As noted by Hutt *et al.* (1990: 195) when reviewing the impact of adult intervention on children's imaginative development:

> Wilson's (1980) study shows, as did the studies by Anderson (1980) and Hughes (1981) . . . that whether the adult uses fantasy or not in her interaction with the child is not important. What is important is that the child is stimulated by the adult to interact with materials and to engage in conversation.

Responses in some cases did go beyond the conversational stage, with practitioners remaining with children at the location of construction materials for extended periods, suggesting and modelling new configurations of the materials, highlighting features of children's constructions to other children in the group and discussing the story lines that children proposed to enact with their constructions.

Others followed up, as detailed in Chapter 5, by providing technology resources, themed small world play or supported fantasy play to build on children's interests.

Comment 12 is a sample from an extended sequence of responses coordinated between practitioners, which provides us with a more substantial example of valuing and extending children's war, weapon and superhero play, and we will now look at this in a little more detail.

Jasper's story

The sequence begins when Jasper, a 3-year-old boy with a consuming interest in weapons and adventure play but no history of aggressive behaviour, constructs a large-scale and elaborate 'laser gun' from Connexion. Jasper has not yet developed a network of friends and often plays alone, frequently with construction, but he also enjoys dressing up and will often don a cloak to role-play a character from an adventure video, for example Zorro. Jan, a practitioner, spots him trying out his construction across the playground and approaches him with a grin, commenting on the scale and complexity of his construction, and asks him about some of the features.

Jasper tells her that it is a laser gun and shows her how it fits snugly over his shoulder. He offers her a turn and corrects the way she holds it when she takes it from him. Jan asks him how he managed to make it and he offers to show her. As he begins to construct, with Jan helping by holding some pieces in place under his direction, he declares that this model is a 'shaker bubble'. Jasper has decided not to repeat his previous construction. As the model progresses Jasper begins to verbalize and demonstrate how different bits work; for example, he grasps two side projections and vibrates them vigorously to show how the bubbles are shaken, perhaps utilizing knowledge from bath time or washing up time that agitation produces bubbles from detergents. He also talks about 'getting the baddies'. Although his construction has diverged from the earlier laser gun, the notion of a weapon is still present in the 'shaker bubble' but is undergoing an imaginative transformation.

Jasper is supported in this activity for nearly ten minutes and the involved presence of Jan also draws a number of other children over to see what is happening. Her obvious admiration for Jasper's skills enhances his social capital. As tidying up time approaches Jan asks Jasper if he would like to keep his construction to show the other children at carpet time and his mum at home time. Jasper smiles, visibly excited and flattered.

Jan carefully carries the construction inside and hands it over to Amina, who is leading carpet time, taking time to brief her about the sustained effort and imaginative accompanying narrative that Jasper has made. Amina continues the sensitive responses that Jan has been making, helps Jasper carry his 'shaker bubble' into the carpeted area and gently guides Jasper and the other children into a discussion about the construction. Jasper demonstrates how to shake the construction and, pointing towards the front, tells the children that 'chocolate bubbles come out of these holes and make the ghost dead'.

Jasper's narrative develops with the telling and in response to the comments of the other children. One little girl, Amy, is very concerned about the idea of ghosts getting chocolate, even if it makes them dead. 'You're not going to let ghosts have chocolate, because they're naughty. Only good people get chocolate. I get chocolate when I'm good.' Jasper ponders for a moment and then reassures Amy that the ghosts will only get 'bad chocolate'.

This supported dialogue with peers increases Jasper's standing in the group, creates a rich language context for using and extending an imaginative narrative arising from weapon construction and enables Jasper to reflect on and refine his thinking. Was his response to Amy an example of theory of mind in operation (Lewis and Mitchell 1994) insofar as he acted to acknowledge her anxiety and to soothe it, or was it more a case of Jasper adjusting his magical thinking to be more consistent with the workings of reality as highlighted by Amy?

Construction, narrative and literacy

The potential significance of construction play for the development of narrative and pre-literacy skills in boys is explored by Kate Pahl:

> Model making can be a response to a thought already present in children's minds, or the thought can be created as the model is made. Many boys' narratives developed pictorially, in response to what they saw on the page or at the modelling table. This way of seeing the world, of expressing meaning firstly in the visual/spatial medium, is significant. Model making may be a way into communication for some boys. If we apply Vygotsky's model of 'inner speech' we might conclude that in the initial stages of formulating an idea, some boys use non-linguistic forms such as models to describe what they are trying to say. The domain of space provides a better reflection of their inner thoughts than

that of language. When literacy is something a child feels to be accessible, the domain of the third dimension, such as the curve of a piece of cut-out cardboard, provides a space in which to make meaning.

(1999: 90)

Models constructed of Lego or Duplo may be dismantled without ever being interpreted or 'read' correctly by an adult. The activities boys do, including construction activities, need to be valued as activities of equal value to girls' narratives.

(1999: 92)

I have dwelt on construction activities in this chapter because we often seem to treat them as a minor aspect of creative and imaginative play. Generally we see construction activities as merely promoting fine motor skills, keeping the boys happy and settled while we attend to those areas that we see as more cognitively productive, like the writing table or maths area.

To close this section I will refer to the work of Frank Smith (1982), who saw literacy as developing along two parallel pathways: transcription – the secretarial or physical act of writing, and composition – the creative act of generating narrative. His work was attacked with the introduction of the Education Reform Act (ERA) in 1988, but ironically these two strands have re-emerged in didactic forms in the literacy strategy early writing document. However, this latter sees the role of adults as teaching children directly both transcription skills and how to be imaginative. In contrast, Smith felt that young children acquiring literacy needed to be supported independently across these aspects of writing so that they could compose at greater length and with greater fluidity than they could physically manage to write independently. Scribing for young children, writing down a caption or story to a child's dictation, was one of the support strategies he advocated.

His work meshes with that of Kate Pahl (1999) in the way that she cites construction activities as providing a compositional link for some young boys into literacy and reminds us that construction activities can simultaneously support both the transcription skills needed for literacy through the development of fine motor skills and the imaginative skills of composition which current formal approaches to literacy can sometimes devalue.

The chase is on

In the final part of this chapter we will look at what children do with their constructions once they have made them. In all settings I have observed children approaching weapon construction in a variety of ways. Some children will set about construction alone, in pairs or small groups, with a clear play scenario in mind for which they are constructing props. This will be evident from either their shared dialogue, 'Come on we're going to get the baddies', 'OK . . . I'm going to be Batman, you be Robin' or their body language, looking around for a play partner or leaving the construction area on tiptoe to find an imaginary baddie to stalk.

For other children the act of construction will have a more primary role, with discussion or solitary speech focused around the detail of the weapon and its properties. Often solitary boys and, notably, girls would appear to be waiting for more experienced peers to take the lead in the ensuing play and would take their cues from them. A storyline might start to unfold, as in small world play, while children are still in the construction area and this chapter will conclude with a particularly striking example of how construction activities can flow into extended socio-dramatic narrative.

We will first, however, look at what is perhaps the most common pattern of development of the play, especially in settings in the early stages of changing policy. Children will most frequently leave the construction area to embark on simple chasing or circuit running games. Often children will head off initially in pursuit of fantasy foes and this is a feature that consistently struck me: children rarely depended on another child or group of children to take on the role of the enemy in order to enter their play scenario.

This was equally true in settings where a ban on shooting at others was maintained and those where children were allowed to shoot at consenting playmates. This is perhaps particularly important in view of the anxieties expressed by some practitioners that some children might become victimized by always being cast in the role of the baddie. There were examples of children ambushing others not involved in their play scenario, but these incidents diminished where children were empowered to say no and where this boundary was actively enforced by adults.

My impression of these fantasy chases is that they often followed a straight-line trajectory with children chasing an imaginary foe in one direction and then running back, imagining that they were being pursued. A frequent development from this would occur as more children joined in and two play groups chasing each other in a circular route emerged. The use of these different trajectories is a tentative observation from my analysis of video evidence and requires further research to confirm the occurrence and relevance of such patterns, but it is a feature that practitioners reading this book may wish to look out for.

These chases were always characterized by laughter and reciprocal turn taking, with the direction of the chase being frequently reversed. Consistent with the evidence from researchers examining play fighting, rough and tumble and physically active play, girls were frequent participants in these play bouts (Pellegrini and Smith 1998). Incidents of uncontrolled physical contact or conflict between children arising from this play were extremely rare.

Sometimes within the same play session and sometimes over a period of weeks a greater level of pretend would become evident in these chases. This would take the form of more specific characterization of the baddie as burglar, monster, dangerous animal or character from the media, and the incorporation of dens or hiding places on the circuit like climbing frames, play houses or trees and bushes. These would be used to heighten the imaginative possibilities of the chase like capture, escape and rescue. Such sophistications of the chase would require an increasing degree of coordination and collaboration between the groups of children participating. Sometimes weapons would retain an important role but often their importance would diminish as other elements of the play developed. This is strikingly similar to Blurton-Jones's (1967) observations in developments within rough-and-tumble play (p.356):

> Rough-and-tumble play subsequently seems to develop rather sharply into formalized games like 'tag' and 'cowboys and Indians'. There are the same motor patterns but rules and verbal explanations have been added.

Chase games of this sort have long been recognized as a common and distinctive aspect of young children's play, particularly by ethologists (Blurton-Jones 1967), those interested in comparative studies of primate and human behaviour, and psychologists concerned with patterns and meaning in children's behaviour (Pellegrini and Smith 1998). Clearly these games exist independently of war, weapon and superhero play, kiss chase being another example of this play format, but my observations indicate both that chase games are often discouraged in settings where zero tolerance is in force and that they flourish where zero tolerance has been relaxed.

One practitioner, in a questionnaire response, said that she had decided to reinstate zero tolerance because when she had relaxed it children *just* run around with their weapons (my emphasis).

While the meaning and value of this play form and whether it fits in the category of physical activity play or rough and tumble remains the subject of debate, I feel that we need to attend to, rather than dismiss, patterns in play that persist across time and place and to seek meaning through observation and interaction. Descriptions of the features of this play from Blurton-Jones's (1967) early investigations, which so closely match the observations I have made in my own study, support this call for practitioners to value and investigate this persistent aspect of children's play culture.

> The human 'rough-and-tumble play', as I shall call it . . . consists of seven movement patterns which tend to occur at the same time as each other and not to occur with other movements. These are running, chasing and fleeing; wrestling; jumping up and down with both feet together . . .; beating at each other with an open hand without actually hitting . . .; beating at each other with an object but not hitting; laughing. In addition, falling seems to be a regular part of this behaviour, and if there is anything soft to land on children spend much time throwing themselves and each other on to it.
>
> (Blurton-Jones 1967: 355)

I have observed a variety of supportive responses made by practitioners to this aspect of children's play: planning the layout of playground equipment to facilitate and protect both those involved and those not involved in chasing games; providing tunnel circuits in the classroom; reorganizing furniture and helping children to develop an appropriate movement vocabulary like crawling and tiptoeing to facilitate this form of play inside the classroom; constructing dens with children; joining in the chase sequence in pretend capacity; and suggesting new imaginative twists to the narrative like the use of magic tokens rather than guns to immobilize the baddies in the chase.

Journey of the heart

Alongside these more obvious patterns of individual and collaborative construction and group chase games there are also examples of children developing imaginative play sequences, which depart from their origins in war, weapon and superhero play. These sequences attract less attention and only come to our notice when we tune in and track the play. As promised earlier, this chapter concludes with a description of such a sequence, which I hope will leave the reader with a sense of the rich narrative potential of war, weapon and superhero play as providing a gateway for children to enter imaginary worlds, which might otherwise be closed to them.

> Magnus is playing by himself on the carpet with Mobilo, constructing a car. His friend Jon arrives in the classroom, rushes over to Magnus shouting, 'Go, go Power Rangers', he aims a few karate kicks and punches into the air and finally throws himself onto the carpet next to Magnus. Had zero tolerance been in force Jon would have been 'intercepted' mid-karate kick and probably spirited off by a practitioner to be supervised into a more 'settled' activity. Happily it was not, and the sequence was allowed to develop.
>
> Jon joined Magnus in constructing a car and started to talk to Magnus about what he was making, 'See, it's his car and now [circling the car in the air] it's going to be a plane . . . neeow . . . and now it's going to be a car again.' He was utilizing the transformatory powers common to superhero scenarios in the narrative accompanying his construction play. After about ten minutes of settled collaborative construction and storying in this vein the doors were opened for outdoor play and Magnus and Jon ran out, leaving their constructions on the carpet.
>
> They headed for a small covered corner of the playground, having grabbed a cushion en route as a seat, and continued the theme of the car which turns into a plane. They have expanded the degree of imaginative involvement by placing themselves inside the car/plane. The stream of language is by now flowing between the two children. Magnus asks if the plane is going to Iceland, his homeland. He is having a difficult time at home and Iceland represents security. Jon presses some imaginary buttons to make the plane take off; they land, jump out and debate whether they are yet in Iceland, run off down the playground and continue their journey in another plane (underneath a picnic bench), but before they get to Iceland they have to go to ''Copalypse Way'.
>
> The play continued in this way for 40 minutes. Magnus is able to take his best friend on a visit to his homeland, which although physically distant can be brought emotionally and imaginatively within reach through the dramatic device of the transformatory Power Rangers car. At no point in this sequence did either child use any aggressive language or behaviour. At no other time had these children been observed in such an extended play sequence.

7

CONCLUSION

Whenever I speak to a group of practitioners about my perspectives on war, weapon and superhero play, the first thing I stress is that I am not trying to offer a neatly packaged alternative strategy to zero tolerance of this area of play. I emphasize that my chief aim is to promote reflection on policy, practice and personal and professional attitudes towards war, weapon and superhero play in particular and towards gender work in early childhood in general.

This is the central point that I wish to emphasize in the closing pages of this book.

It is tempting in all areas of our personal and professional lives to look for straightforward, clear-cut answers to our questions and to put our faith in the views of experts in any given field. However, from an academic perspective, one of the key things I have learnt as my knowledge becomes more specialized is that the more I come to understand of the nature of war, weapon and superhero play the more I appreciate how much more there is to explore and learn. This book has explored the visible tip of the iceberg and has offered some informed analytical views about what may be going on underneath the surface for both children and practitioners.

All research work concerning young children is dependent on observations of that part of the childhood iceberg we can see, hear, measure and compare. No two icebergs and no two children are the same and no two observers will see the same child in quite the same way. However, if we observe numbers of children over time, patterns of similarity and difference will emerge. These patterns may be analysed differently by two observers influenced by different theoretical perspectives. If, however, the observers enter a dialogue with each other and understand that their view is just one among a range of diverse perspectives it is likely that they will jointly come up with a more comprehensive view of the child.

This does not mean that we should just randomly pluck the bits we like from different views of the child, but rather that we should be aware of what influences our own views of children and be prepared to challenge that view and analyse children's behaviour from different theoretical frameworks. There is no absolute known truth about how children develop and learn and the body of knowledge and understanding grows and changes constantly.

Within this book I have engaged in a written dialogue with some of those who have thought, researched and written about war, weapon and superhero play or related issues. It would be impossible within one book to review comprehensively all of the relevant material, and dishonest to claim that the material that does appear has been selected and presented in a clinically neutral way. All researchers and writers have a standpoint, a perspective, which informs their work and the way in which they relate to the work of others. Our notions of academic integrity are generally associated with the concepts of objectivity, the neutral observer and proof.

When I was seeking to extend my research from the initial setting, discussed in Chapter 4, I was dogged by those ideas. How could I design a piece of research to test whether the finding from that setting could be generalized to other early years settings?

> A generalisation is prized precisely because, in not being limited to a particular setting, it is seen as making application possible. Thus, generalisations have been traditionally considered the highest level of research and very often as what research should always strive for. This is largely because research in the natural sciences, particularly in physics, aims for generalisations and such research is thought to be the model for all other forms of research. In the natural sciences generalisations are sought because they enable predictions to be made . . . Not why does x happen in this particular classroom but does it happen in all classrooms and if so is there an underlying and common cause y?
>
> (Usher 1996: 10)

How could I measure the benefits of relaxing zero tolerance of war, weapon and superhero play for those children with a persistent interest in that area of play? How could I prove that war, weapon and superhero play does not lead to aggressive behaviour?

Ultimately I realized that I could not do any of these to my satisfaction, because I could not hope to remove the layers of variables which exist in the daily life of an early childhood setting, and because the area to be investigated rests on subjectivities: my own; those of the children and those of the practitioners in the settings. Zero tolerance is an approach that has itself been produced by an interplay of subjectivities. It has been sustained historically because it has resonance with the subjectivities of the female workforce, largely as a result of their personal perceptions of war, weapon and superhero play as germinal male violence and/or because they have absorbed an unquestioning approach to policy as a result of the low status of their work. This approach has been applied within the framework of the dynamics of the personal and professional interface with the subjectivities of young children (almost exclusively male) who have, for a variety of reasons, a persistent interest in this area of play. My subjectivity intrudes here – as a practitioner, who vigorously supported zero tolerance from a feminist perspective, and as an academic, who subsequently felt obliged to re-examine my position because of the negative impact it was having on children in my care.

To put it in a nutshell, policy and practice in relation to war, weapon and superhero play is dependent on a complex weave of feelings, attitudes, relationships and perceptions, and research in this area needs to take account of this complexity rather than seek to neutralize it.

While some of the more statistically based studies reported in this book can usefully inform our thinking in this area, they need to be regarded as part of the picture rather than the whole canvas. For example, the studies of practitioners' perceptions of play fighting considered in Chapter 2 (Connor 1989; Schafer and Smith 1996) alert us to the need to be reflective about our attitudes, but they do not tell us what impact these attitudes have on children. The work of Dunn and Hughes (2001) alerts us to a relationship between the incidence of violent play themes at age 4 and anti-social behaviour at age 6, but does not tell us about policy and practice towards those play themes in the settings researched or the possibility of working with those children to change the outcomes observed. Those who support zero tolerance could use this latter piece of research to support an argument that war, weapon and superhero play leads to aggressive behaviour, whereas the work shows an associative but not causal connection. None of the research used in the area of imaginative play conclusively proves that development in this area will lead to better conflict resolution skills, but rather points towards such a connection.

I have dwelt upon these issues because I do not wish this book to be viewed as a guide to changing practice in relation to war, weapon and superhero play but rather as a prompt to reflection and increasingly diverse practice in this area. My experience of observing practice in different settings has made me appreciate in a far deeper way that the standardization of practice is an unachievable and dubious goal and, equally, that the route to change will be different in each setting.

For example, in Chapters 4 and 5 we looked at the issue of boundaries and whether children should be allowed to point and shoot constructed weapons at each other. Different settings had established different boundaries in this area depending on the views and feelings of the practitioners and in some the views of the children were being sought. I argued that there should be no absolute right or wrong in relation to this boundary because practitioners need to feel committed to, and comfortable with, the operation of any boundary.

The possibility of change in some settings has been ruled out because the team is split in its view of zero tolerance and it has been felt that the acrimony and tension which might follow if change were to be enforced would limit any benefits the change might bring because some practitioners would refuse to interact and extend the play. This situation arose in one setting that I worked with and, although individual children seemed to benefit from the change, specifically Darren, whom we met in Chapter 3, I do not believe children in that setting enjoyed the full range of benefits enjoyed by those in settings where the policy change was fully supported. Some members of this team were also relatively inexperienced and had little confidence in developing children's imaginative play. Consequently the rest of the team members struggled to work responsively with the play and some pre-existing tensions between members of the team were made worse. It might have been of more benefit to children in that setting if the team had focused on team building and developing imaginative play before embarking on changing their zero tolerance policy.

Another way in which practitioners could respond to the material in this book would be to review the genderscape in their classrooms in a general way, including the operation of approaches to war, weapon and superhero play, and to conclude that they would continue with zero tolerance while developing their attitudes and curriculum in other ways to support the interests of boys and develop more active play for girls.

A range of wider community issues might also determine policy and practice in relation to war, weapon and superhero play. It would be very difficult, for example, to relax zero tolerance in a situation where a number of parents/carers expressed objections. On a different level, communities that have experienced armed conflict or school shootings as in Northern Ireland or Dunblane might well, unsurprisingly, find it impossible to countenance a relaxation of zero tolerance. Some practitioners have argued that some refugee children newly arrived in England may have a need to represent their experiences of military conflict, while others have pointed out that some children may need to be protected from play scenarios which could trigger traumatic memories. Similarly, it can be argued that children of families serving in the armed forces should feel as free to represent the occupations and tools of their parent's occupation as the children of plumbers or teachers. Cultural contexts clearly need to be considered when determining policy and practice in relation to war, weapon and superhero play.

These cultural considerations also fuel my conviction that it is not appropriate to fix policy and practice universally in relation to war, weapon and superhero play, in the way that zero tolerance has done, on the basis of a moral conviction that all representations of aggression and violence are unacceptable and potentially, or probably, damaging. To act from such a conviction while children are surrounded by images and experiences of both real and fantasy violence and aggression generated by adults seems to be an act of ostrich-like hypocrisy.

We may disassociate ourselves from these acts, but surely we cannot avoid taking responsibility in a broader social sense for supporting children in dealing with such images and events. If we are to continue to apply zero tolerance in our settings then we urgently need to work out how we will offer this support: children cannot simply empty their minds at the classroom door nor, as Jasper's story in Chapter 6 shows, can we simply pour peaceful thoughts into their heads to replace their fears, anxieties and need to feel safe. Relaxing zero tolerance and working with children's imaginative development may not be a culturally or pragmatically appropriate response in all cases, but unmediated zero tolerance simply seems to offer adults a way to avoid dealing both with children's needs and the bigger social issues underpinning them.

Another strand of moral argument that I wish to add concerns the proverbial statement that 'peace cannot be achieved by force, but only by understanding'. Zero tolerance relies on the use of adult power in the real world to enforce a moral and behavioural imperative against powerless children operating in a fantasy world. I found myself reflecting on this interpretation of zero tolerance of war, weapon and superhero play repeatedly in the days following 11 September.

Despite my feelings of shock and terror at these events I found myself equally disturbed and terrified by the bellicose response of the governments of the USA and England. How could threatening to visit death and destruction on the inhabitants of another part of the world be considered acceptable retribution for the loss of life in the World Trade Center towers? The script and language of revenge sounded remarkably similar from both sides of the divide. I was as frightened for the future of our world by the escalation threatened by those represented as the good guys as by the horrendous acts of those represented as the bad guys. Meeting force with force generates an unending spiral of resistance and revenge of which the events of 11 September were no more a beginning than the fall of the Taliban was an end. The issue for me was the scale and abuse of power on both sides. There was no right or wrong side in that power equation.

To return these thoughts to the microcosm of the classroom I understood anew just how carefully we need to model the use of power in our relationships with children. We have power and must use it wisely. Using our physical power or moral authority to prevent children from hurting themselves or others must be viewed as an acceptable use of that power, but to use our power to colonize their fantasy worlds is surely heading down the road of control and compliance in an altogether different direction. If we subject them to our authority at that level do we not perhaps run the risk of teaching children to resist us, to assert their autonomy at any cost or, alternatively, to comply to whoever holds greatest power in their circle at different times in their lives? If, however, we use our power sparingly and reflectively, might we not teach children that it is possible to negotiate across difference and that force against force is not the only response to conflict?

Jerome Singer (1994: 24–5) has expressed similar thoughts.

> While I certainly do not wish to propose that providing millions of children with toy soldier sets would alleviate real violence in the world and generate pacifism, I do want to emphasize that such toys can be conducive to generating imaginative play without provoking overtly violent behaviour. I am much more concerned about the millions of children who have no toys, no parents who tell stories or read to them, and no sense of history but who do have available *real* guns and who are stimulated to imitation by older peers and by the heavy doses of daily exposure to realistic violence on television. It could be argued that one reason some children act out aggressive behaviour directly (in addition to imitating the adult violence they may experience in the family or vicariously) is that they have not had sufficient development of their own narrative and metarepresentational skills early on. That is, they have not practised, starting with pretend play, their capacity to play out possibilities and situations in a miniaturized mental world,

and by so doing learned to explore negative as well as positive consequences of linking direct actions to wishes and emotions.

To complete the journey upon which I hope I have taken the readers of this book I would like to take us full circle and return to two statements made in the Preface.

I hope that readers will see this book both as offering both new ways of reading war, weapon and superhero play specifically and also as a validation of the important role that small-scale action research by practitioners in early childhood settings can play in expanding our knowledge, understanding and responses to children's play.

My intent is not to change minds, but rather to open them and to fuel debate within the early childhood community in relation to zero tolerance of war, weapon and superhero play, which I believe has become a stagnant area of policy and practice.

> If I have not yet learned to love Darth Vader, I have at least made some useful discoveries while watching him at play. As I interrupt less, it becomes clear that boys' play is serious drama, not morbid mischief. Its rhythms and images are often discordant to me, but I must try to make sense of a style that, after all, belongs to half the population of the classroom.
>
> (Paley 1984: xii)

APPENDIX

Name of contact person...

Name of setting ....

Address...

....

Description of setting (LEA/private/voluntary/number and ages of children/local authority)

....

....

Tel. No...

Email address ....

Question 1 Did you change policy in relation to war, weapon and superhero play in your setting following the workshop you attended? **Yes/No** Please state reasons for making change opposite.	

Question 2 If no change has yet been made do you propose to change policy in the future? **Yes/No**	Whatever your response, would you be interested in further discussion about participating in a research project to record either change, or the ongoing operation of your current policy? **Yes/No**
Question 3 If <u>no</u> change made please state reasons briefly opposite and return form in envelope provided. If you have made changes please answer questions below.	
Question 4 Describe policy before changes.	
Question 5 Describe current policy.	
Question 6 Have these changes been sustained? **Yes/No** Please add additional comments about time span, why you continued with change or didn't.	
Question 7 Would you say that the changes made have been positive overall? **Yes/No** Please comment and give examples.	

Question 8 If there was/is a group of children with a persistent interest in war, weapon and superhero play, please state approximately how many, their ages and gender.	
Question 9 Have you observed any changes in the well-being, behaviour, play, and overall development of these children since changing policy? **Yes/No** Please describe these changes in as much detail as possible. Summaries of individual (anonymous) children would be very helpful, or these could be discussed at a meeting (cont. on separate sheet if necessary).	
Question 10 Have you observed any changes in girls' interest and involvement in war, weapon and superhero play since changing policy? **Yes/No** Please describe.	
Question 11 Do you think there is more or less war, weapon and superhero play since changing policy? **More/Less/Don't Know** Please comment.	
Question 12 Do you think changing policy has had any effect on levels of real aggression of violent play? Please comment.	
Question 13 Did you experience any difficulties in the process of changing policy? **Yes/No** Please give examples.	

Question 14	Please give me some indication
Would you be prepared to meet with me to discuss your experiences in greater depth? **Yes/No** *I will come to you.*	below about time and day of week

Monday	Tuesday	Wednesday	Friday
am	am	am	am
N/A	pm	N/A	pm

pm includes meetings after 3.30

Any other comments?	

THANKS

BIBLIOGRAPHY

Arnot, M., David, M. and Weiner, G. (1999) *Closing the Gender Gap: Postwar Education and Social Change*. Cambridge: Polity Press.

Arsenio, W.F and Lover, A. (1997) Emotions, conflicts and aggression during preschoolers' freeplay, *British Journal of Developmental Psychology*, 15: 531–42.

Askew, S. and Ross, C. (1988) *Boys Don't Cry: Boys and Sexism in Education*. Milton Keynes: Open University Press.

Athey, C. (1990) *Extending Thought in Young Children*. London: Paul Chapman Publishing.

Barrs, M. and Pidgeon, S. (eds) (1998) *Boys and Reading*. London: Language Matters, CLPE.

Berk, L. (1994) Vygotsky's theory: the importance of make-believe play, *Young Children*, November: 30–9.

Berkowitz, L. (1974) Some determinants of impulsive aggression: role of mediated associations with reinforcements for aggression, *Psychological Review*, 81: 165–76.

Bettelheim, B. (1978) *The Uses of Enchantment*. London: Penguin.

Biblow, E. (1973) Imaginative play and the control of aggressive behavior, in J.L. Singer (ed.) *The Child's World of Make Believe: Experimental Studies of Imaginative Play*. New York, NY: Academic Press.

Biddulph, S. (1997) *Raising Boys*. London: Thorsons.

Blurton-Jones, N. (1967) An ethological study of some aspects of social behaviour of children in nursery school, in D. Morris (ed.) *Primate Ethology*, 347–68. London: Weidenfeld and Nicolson.

Bowlby, J. (1969) *Attachment and Loss*, Vol. 1. London: Pimlico.

Broadhead, P. (1992) Play-fighting, play or fighting? – from parallel to co-operative play in the pre-school, *Early Years*, 13(1): 45–9.

Brostrom, S. (1996) Frame play with 6 year-old children, *European Early Childhood Education Research Journal*, 4(1): 89–101.

Browne, N. and France, P. (eds) (1986) *Untying the Apron Strings: Anti-sexist Provision for the Under-Fives*. Milton Keynes: Open University Press.

Brownmiller, S. (1975) *Against Our Will: Men, Women and Rape*. New York, NY: Bantam Books.

Bruce, T. (1991) *Time to Play in Early Childhood Education*. London: Hodder and Stoughton.

Bruce, T. (1996) *Tuning Into Children*. London: BBC Educational Developments.

Bruce, T. (1997a) *Early Childhood Education*, 2nd edn. London: Hodder and Stoughton.

Bruce, T. (1997b) Adults and children developing play together, *European Early Childhood Education Research Journal*, 5(1): 89–99.

Bruner, J. (1966) *Towards a Theory of Instruction*. Cambridge, MA: Belknap Press of Harvard University Press.

Bruner, J. (1986) *Actual Minds, Possible Worlds*. Cambridge, MA: Harvard University Press.

Cameron, C., Moss, P. and Owen, C. (1999) *Men in the Nursery: Gender and Caring Work*. London: Paul Chapman Publishing.

Carlsson-Paige, N. and Levin, D.E. (1990) *Who's Calling the Shots? How to Respond Effectively to Children's Fascination with War Play and War Toys*. Philadelphia, PA: New Society Publishers.

Carlsson-Paige, N. and Levin, D.E. (1995) Can teachers resolve the war-play dilemma?, *Young Children*, July: 62–3.

Carvalho, A.M.A., Smith, P.K., Hunter, T. and Costabile, A. (1990) Playground activities for boys and girls: developmental and cultural trends in children's perceptions of gender differences, *Play and Culture*, 3: 343–7.

Chandler, D. (1997) Children's understanding of what is 'real' on television: a review of the literature, *Journal of Educational Media*, 23(1): 65–80.

Cohen, L. and Manion, L. (1994) *Research Methods in Education*, 4th edn. London: Routledge.

Coie, J.D., Dodge, K.A., Terry, R. and Wright, V. (1991) The role of aggression in peer relations: an analysis of aggression episodes in boys' play groups, *Child Development*, 62: 812–26.

Coles, R. (1997) *The Moral Intelligence of Children*. London: Bloomsbury Publishing Co.

Connell, R.W. (1995) *Masculinities*. Cambridge: Polity Press.

Connor, K. (1989) Aggression: is it in the eye of the beholder?, *Play and Culture*, 2: 213–17.

Convery, A. (1999) Listening to teachers' stories: are we sitting too comfortably?, *Qualitative Studies in Education*, 12(2): 131–46.

Costabile, A., Smith, P.K., Matheson, L. *et al.* (1991) Cross-national comparison of how children distinguish serious and playful fighting, *Developmental Psychology*, 27(5): 881–7.

Cranny-Francis, A. (1992) *Engendered Fictions*. Sydney: University Press.

Cupit, G.C. (1996) Superhero play and very human children, *Early Years*, 16(2): 22–5.

Dahlberg, G., Moss, P. and Pence, A. (1999) *Beyond Quality in Early Childhood Education and Care: Postmodern Perspectives*. London: Falmer Press.

Davies, B. (1989) *Frogs and Snails and Feminist Tales: Preschool Children and Gender*. Sydney: Allen & Unwin.

Dawson, G. (1990) Playing at war: an autobiographical approach to boyhood fantasy and masculinity, *Oral History*, Spring: 44–53.

Dias, M.G. and Harris, P.L. (1990) The influence of the imagination on reasoning by young children, *British Journal of Developmental Psychology*, 8: 305–18.

Doliopoulou, E. (1998) Preschool children's war play: how do Greek teachers and parents cope with it?, *European Early Childhood Education Research Journal*, 6(1): 73–86.

Donaldson, M. (1978) *Children's Minds*. London: Fontana Press.

Dunn, J. (1988) *The Beginning of Social Understanding*. Oxford: Blackwell.

Dunn, J. and Hughes, C. (2001) 'I got some swords and you're dead': violent fantasy, antisocial behaviour, friendship, and moral sensibility in young children, *Child Development*, 72(2): 491–505.

Ebbeck, M. (1998) Gender in early childhood revisited, *Australian Journal of Early Childhood*, 23(1): 29–32.

Evershed, J. (1994) Reflections on young children's role-play: possible insights into their perceptions of the social, *Research in Education*, 51 (May): 67–77.

Fleer, M. (1998) Me not a boy, me a person!: deconstructing gendered interactional patterns in early childhood, *Australian Journal of Early Childhood*, 23(1): 22–7.

Francis, B. (1998) *Power Plays: Primary School Children's Constructions of Gender, Power and Adult Work*. Stoke on Trent: Trentham Books.

Francis, D. (1997) Critical incident analysis: a strategy for developing reflective practice, *Teachers and Teaching: Theory and Practice*, 3(2): 169–87.

Ginn, K. and Warren, M. (2000) Nursery Crime?, *The Scotsman*, 24 May.

Golden, J. (1996) Critical imagination: serious play with narrative and gender, *Gender and Education*, 8(3): 323–35.

Goleman, D. (1996) *Emotional Intelligence*. London: Bloomsbury Publishing.

Greenberg, J. (1995) Making friends with the Power Rangers, *Young Children*, July: 60–61.

Greenfield, S. (1997) *The Human Brain: A Guided Tour*. London: Weidenfeld and Nicolson.

Greenfield, S. (1999) The state of the art of the science of brain research. Unpublished paper presented at Learning and the Brain Day Conference, London, The Royal Institution, 23 November.

Grieshaber, S. (1998) Constructing the gendered infant, in N. Yelland (ed.) *Gender in Early Childhood*, pp. 15–35. London: Routledge.

Gulbenkian Foundation (1995) *Children and Violence: Report of the Commission on Children and Violence Convened by the Gulbenkian Foundation*. London: Calouste Gulbenkian Foundation.

Gurian, M. (2001) *Boys and Girls Learn Differently: A Guide for Teachers and Parents*. San Francisco, CA: Jossey-Bass.

Harbin, J. and Miller, D. (1991) Violent play behavior and language of four-year old boys: the significance of teacher mediation, *Early Child Development and Care*, 75: 79–86.

Harris, P. (2000) *The Work of the Imagination*. Oxford: Blackwell.

Harrison, S. (2000) cited in J. Napier, *Gun Laws*.

Head, J. (1999) *Understanding the Boys*. London: Falmer Press.

Henry, J. (2000) Nursery Declares Truce, *Times Educational Supplement*, 19 May.

Holland, P. (1999a) Just pretending, *Language Matters*, Spring: 2–5.

Holland, P. (1999b) Is zero tolerance intolerance?, *Early Childhood Practice*, 1(1): 65–72.

Holland, P. (2000) Take the toys from the boys? An examination of the genesis of policy and the appropriateness of adult perspectives in the area of war, weapon and superhero play, *Children's Social and Economics Education*, 4(2): 92–108.

Hutt, J., Tyler, S., Hutt, C. and Christopherson, H. (1990) *Play, Exploration and Learning: A Natural History of the Pre-school*. London: Routledge.

ILEA (Inner London Education Authority) (1985) *Race, Sex and Class 6. A Policy for Equality: Sex*. London: Inner London Education Authority.

ILEA (1986) *First Reflections: Equal Opportunities in the Early Years*. London: Inner London Education Authority.

Jackson, D. (1998) Breaking out of the binary trap, in D. Epstein, J. Elwood, V. Hey and J. Maw (eds) *Failing Boys: Issues in Gender and Achievement*, 77–95. Buckingham: Open University Press.

Jones, L. (1996) Young girls' notions of femininity, *Gender and Education*, 8(3): 311–21.

Jordan, E. (1995) Fighting boys and fantasy play: the construction of masculinity in the early years of school, *Gender and Education*, 7(1): 69–86.

Kimura, D. (2000) *Sex and Cognition*. Cambridge, MA: MIT Press.

Kohlberg, L. (1966) A cognitive developmental analysis of children's sex role concepts and attitudes, in E.E. Maccoby (ed.) *The Development of Sex Differences*, pp. 57–8. Stanford, CA: Stanford University Press.

Kuykendall, J. (1995) Is gun play OK here???, *Young Children*, 50(5): 56–59.

Laevers, F., Vandenbussche, E., Kog, M. and Depondt, L. (1997) *A Process Oriented Child Monitoring System for Young Children*. Experiential Education Series No. 2. Leuven, Belgium: Centre for Experiential Education.

Lawrence, D. (1988) *Enhancing Self-Esteem in the Classroom*. London: Paul Chapman Publishing.

Lewis, C. and Mitchell, P. (eds) (1994) *Children's Early Understanding of Mind*. Hove: Lawrence Erlbaum Associates.

Lloyd, B. (1990) Social representations of gender, in J. Bruner and H. Haste (eds) *Making Sense: The Child's Construction of the World*, pp. 147–162. London: Routledge.

Lloyd, T. (1999) *Reading for the Future: Boys' and Fathers' Views on Reading*. London: Save The Children.

Lyotard, J. (1984) *The Postmodern Condition: A Report on Knowledge*. Manchester: Manchester University Press.

MacNaughton, G. (2000) *Rethinking Gender in Early Childhood Education*. London: Paul Chapman Publishing.

Marsh, J. (1999) Batman and Batwoman go to school: popular culture in the literacy curriculum, *International Journal of Early Years Education*, 7(2): 117–31.

Miedzian, M. (1992) *Boys Will Be Boys*. London: Virago.

Moss, P. and Penn, H. (1996) *Transforming Nursery Education*. London: Paul Chapman Publishing.

Napier, J. (2000) Gun laws, *Nursery World*, 11 May: 11.

NCH (1994) *The Hidden Victims: Children and Domestic Violence*. London: NCH Action For Children.

Orpinas, P., Murray, M., and Kelder, S. (1999) Parental influences on students' aggressive behaviors and weapon carrying, *Health Education and Behavior*, 26(6): 774–87.

O'Sullivan, S. (1980) Thinking about boy children, *Spare Rib*, 96 (July): 26–7.

Pahl, K. (1999) *Transformations: Meaning Making in Nursery Education*. Stoke on Trent: Trentham Books.

Paley, V.G. (1984) *Boys and Girls: Superheroes in the Doll Corner*. Chicago, IL: University of Chicago Press.

Pascal, C., Ramsden, F., Sanders, M. *et al.* (1996) *Evaluating and Developing Quality in Early Childhood Settings: A Professional Development Programme*. Worcester: Amber Publishing Co.

Pellegrini, A.D. (1988) Elementary-school children's rough-and-tumble play and social competence, *Developmental Psychology*, 24(6): 802–6.

Pellegrini, A.D. and Smith, P.K. (1998) Physical activity play: the nature and function of a neglected aspect of play, *Child Development*, 69(3): 577–98.

Piaget, J. (1962) *Play, Dreams and Imitation In Childhood*. London: Routledge and Kegan Paul.

Piaget, J. and Inhelder, B. (1969) *The Psychology of the Child*. London: Routledge and Kegan Paul.

Pizzey, E. (1974) *Scream Quietly or the Neighbours Will Hear*. Harmondsworth: Penguin Books.

Potter, G. (1996) From symbolic play to symbolic representation in early literacy: clarifying the links, *Early Years*, 16(2): 13–16.

QCA (Qualifications and Curriculum Authority) (1998) *Can Do Better: Raising Boys' Achievement in English*. London: QCA Publications.

QCA (2000) *Curriculum Guidance for the Foundation Stage*. London: QCA Publications.

Ramazanoglu, C. (1993) *Up Against Foucault: Explorations of Some Tensions Between Foucault and Feminism*. London: Routledge.

Reay, D. (2001) 'Spice girls', 'nice girls', 'girlies', and 'tomboys': gender discourses, girls' cultures and femininities in the primary classroom, *Gender and Education*, 13(2): 153–66.

Schafer, M. and Smith, P.K. (1996) Teacher's perceptions of play fighting and real fighting in primary school, *Educational Research*, 38(2): 173–81.

Singer, J.L. (1973) (ed.) *The Child's World of Make Believe: Experimental Studies of Imaginative Play*. New York, NY: Academic Press.

Singer, D. and Singer, J. (1990) *The House of Make Believe: Children's Play and the Developing Imagination*. Cambridge, MA: Harvard University Press.

Singer, J.L. (1994) Imaginative play and adaptive development, in J.H. Goldstein (ed.) *Toys, Play and Child Development*. Cambridge: Cambridge University Press.

Smilansky, S. and Shefatya, L. (1990) *Facilitating Play: A Medium for*

Promoting Cognitive, Socio-emotional and Economic Development in Young Children. Silver Spring, Maryland: Psychosocial and Educational Publications.

Smith, C. and Lloyd, B.B. (1978) Maternal behaviour and perceived sex of infant, *Child Development*, 49: 1263–5.

Smith, E. (1994) *Educating the Under-Fives*. London: Cassell.

Smith, F. (1982) *Writing and the Writer*. London: Heinemann Educational Books.

Smith, P.K. (1984) The relevance of fantasy play for development in young children, in H. Cowie (ed.) *The Development of Children's Imaginative Writing*, pp. 12–21. London: Croom Helm.

Sutton-Smith, B. (1986) *Toys as Culture*. New York, NY: Gardner Press.

Sutton-Smith, B. (1988) War toys and childhood aggression, *Play and Culture*, 1: 57–69.

Turner, C.W. and Goldsmith, D. (1976) Effects of toy guns and airplanes on children's antisocial free play behavior, *Journal of Experimental Child Psychology*, 21: 303–15.

Usher, R. (1996) A critique of the neglected epistemological assumptions of educational research, in D. Scott and R. Usher (eds) *Understanding Educational Research*. London: Routledge.

Vygotsky, L. (1978) *Mind In Society*. Cambridge, MA: Harvard University Press.

Walkerdine, V. (1990) *Schoolgirl Fictions*. London: Verso.

Watson, M.W. and Peng, Y. (1992) The relation between toy gun play and children's aggressive behavior, *Early Education and Development*, 3(4): 370–89.

Whyte, J. (1983) *Beyond the Wendy House: Sex Role Stereotyping in Primary Schools*. London: Longman Group.

Yelland, N. (ed.) (1998) *Gender In Early Childhood*. London: Routledge.

INDEX

THE FOUNDATIONS OF LEARNING
Julie Fisher (ed.)

The introduction of the Foundation Stage for children age 3 to becoming 6, has had a profound impact on policy and practice in early education in the UK. The choice of the word 'foundation' to describe this first stage of learning has emphasized the importance of children's earliest experiences in underpinning all their subsequent attitudes and achievements. In this innovative and challenging book, Julie Fisher has brought together some of the country's leading early years specialists to explore how educators can establish firm foundations for young children's learning. The themes in the book are stimulated by the metaphor of 'foundations', with an introduction by an architect who explains the principles of establishing firm foundations for buildings. Each of these established engineering principles is then creatively explored from an educational perspective as the authors seek to question how the foundations laid for buildings can offer fresh insights into the principles for creating firm foundations for learning.

Contents
Introduction: the importance of firm foundations . . . an analogy with architecture – Breadth and depth in early foundations – High levels of achievement for young children – The impact of stress on early development – Meeting the needs of disadvantaged children – Making meaningful connections in early learning – Assessing what matters in the early years – The consequences of inadequate investment in the early years – Conclusions: the foundations of learning – References – Index.

Contributors
Tony Bertram, Adrian Cooper, Marion Dowling, Margaret Edgington, Julie Fisher, Christine Pascal, Linda Pound, Gillian Pugh OBE, Wendy Scott, Pauline Trudell.

158pp   0 335 20991 2 (Paperback)   0 335 20992 0 (Hardback)

SUPPORTING DRAMA AND IMAGINATIVE PLAY IN THE EARLY YEARS

Lesley Hendy and Lucy Toon

Written for the wide range of practitioners working with young children, this book gives guidance on both the theory and the practical management of drama in the Early Years. The relationship between 'pretend play' and the cognitive and affective development of young children is emphasised, having much to inform us about the children in our care. Major themes are children's need to experience quality talk and their engagement in narrative through story-making.

The authors have a wide range of experience in Early Years teaching and in teacher training. Through their work, they are aware of the importance of drama for the development of the young child. Parents and practitioners are encouraged to explore drama activities and examples are given of fantasy play taken from pre-school, nursery and infant settings.

All those involved with Early Years can discover that engaging children in dramatic activity is both a natural form of behaviour and a powerful learning medium.

Contents

176pp   0 335 20665 4 (Paperback)   0 335 20666 2 (Hardback)

DOING EARLY CHILDHOOD RESEARCH
INTERNATIONAL PERSPECTIVES ON THEORY AND PRACTICE

Glenda Mac Naughton, Sharne A. Rolfe and Iram Siraj-Blatchford

Doing Early Childhood Research demystifies the research process. An international team of experienced researchers shows how to select the right questions and use the appropriate methods to investigate important issues in early childhood.

The editors and authors provide a thorough introduction to the most common research methods used in the early childhood context. Reflecting the multidisciplinary nature of much early childhood research, they cover a wide range of conventional and newer approaches including observation, small surveys, action research, ethnography, policy analysis and poststructuralist approaches.

They explain clearly how to set up research projects which are theoretically grounded, well-designed, rigorously analysed, feasible and ethically fair. Each chapter is illustrated with examples and case studies.

Doing Early Childhood Research is essential reading for new researchers and students inexperienced in conducting research.

Contents

Contributors

Liz Brooker, Sheralyn Campbell, Leslie Cannold, Margaret M. Coady, Anne Edwards, Ann Farrell, Susan Grieshaber, Linda Harrison, Alan Hayes, Patrick Hughes, Glenda Mac Naughton, Mindy Blaise Ochsner, Sharne A. Rolfe, Sharon Ryan, Iram Siraj-Blatchford, John Siraj-Blatchford.

320pp   0 335 20902 5 (Paperback)